THE
Red BOOK
OF
BOUNDARIES

RUBY EDITION

TIFFANY BUCKNER

© 2021, Tiffany Buckner
The Red Book of Boundaries
www.tiffanybuckner.com
info@anointedfire.com

Published by:
Anointed Fire™ House
www.anointedfirehouse.com

Cover Design by:
Anointed Fire™ House

Author photograph by:
Photo by: Brand You Brand Nu

Edited by:
Jose Juguna

ISBN: 978-1-7354654-9-4

Note from the Author

Hey you! Thank you for purchasing the Book of Boundaries (Ruby edition). Before you proceed any further into this book series, I want to share my heart with you regarding this series. After having ministered to or counseled countless women about boundary-setting, it became apparent that the issues that are ever-so-prevalent in this world are mainly centered around a need for boundaries. I can truly say that more than ninety percent of the people I've coached, counseled or mentored were in dire straits simply because they didn't have any solid or healthy boundaries set in their lives. In truth, most people have never had anyone to teach them how to properly set boundaries. Consequently, our mental institutions and prisons are overflowing with people whose minds have been taken over by the enemy. All the same, school shootings, racism, divorce, rape, abuse and essentially every evil thing on Earth has been thriving as the human race continues to descend into madness. This is why I created the Book of Boundaries!

You'll notice that there are five parts to this series. They are:
1. The Onyx Edition
2. The Emerald Edition
3. The Sapphire Edition
4. The Jasper Edition
5. **The Ruby Edition** (You are here)

I chose these names for several reasons, but mainly

because of their colors and what those colors represent. All the same, each of these stones could be found in the ephod of the high priest. "Ye have seen what I did unto the Egyptians, and how I bare you on eagles' wings, and brought you unto myself. Now therefore, if ye will obey my voice indeed, and keep my covenant, then ye shall be a peculiar treasure unto me above all people: for all the earth is mine: And ye shall be unto me a kingdom of priests, and an holy nation. These are the words which thou shalt speak unto the children of Israel" (Exodus 19:4-6). Believers are priests or priestesses of the Most High God, and as such, we should not be in bondage to any person or system that is contrary to our design! This means that these books are all about IDENTITY! They will help you to better understand who you are and give you the confidence needed to embrace your God-given identity! Once you do this, it will be easier for you to appreciate yourself enough to establish boundaries.

Each of these books represent your exodus from one mindset to another one. You won't just learn about boundaries, but you will learn a lot about yourself while reading this series! You will learn about demonology, relationships and how the enemy advances against the minds of God's people by simply using the technology of ignorance! You will go from black to blue, from not knowing to understanding why it is necessary for you to set boundaries, what it looks and feels like to live behind boundaries, and what you stand to gain once you effectively set and enforce boundaries in your life. You will learn about the infamous narcissist and how to rid your life of that evil force once and for all. This is a must-have book for the sane and the insane! It is designed to help you to take back the real estate of your mind that the enemy has stolen from you!

In this series, I also shared some of my personal stories and dreams with you so that you can also witness the exodus that I had to take from being a mess to a living message! I shared these stories so that you can know that it is POSSIBLE for you to completely leave and annihilate one mindset and lifestyle, and wholeheartedly embrace another lifestyle that looks NOTHING like the one you left behind!

Welcome to the Book of Boundaries! Warning: revelation produces a paradigmatic shift, which causes things in your life that shouldn't be there to wither up and fall away. In other words, if you like being broken, bound and miserable, don't go any further because the revelation in this series is potent enough to sober you up! But if you're ready for a change, flip the page!

Sincerely,
Tiffany Buckner

Introduction

Scriptures for this Edition

And the LORD said unto Moses, Wherefore criest thou unto me? Speak unto the children of Israel, that they go forward: But lift thou up thy rod, and stretch out thine hand over the sea, and divide it: and the children of Israel shall go on dry ground through the midst of the sea.
Exodus 14:15-16

And Moses stretched out his hand over the sea; and the LORD caused the sea to go back by a strong east wind all that night, and made the sea dry land, and the waters were divided. And the children of Israel went into the midst of the sea upon the dry ground: and the waters were a wall unto them on their right hand, and on their left.
Exodus 14:21-22

And the blood shall be to you for a token upon the houses where ye are: and when I see the blood, I will pass over you, and the plague shall not be upon you to destroy you, when I smite the land of Egypt.
Exodus 12:13

But if we walk in the light, as he is in the light, we have fellowship one with another, and the blood of Jesus Christ his Son cleanseth us from all sin.
1 John 1:7

The ruby stone is RED.

The color red, in this edition, represents deliverance; it represents the blood of Jesus and the power of His blood. It symbolizes crossing the Red Sea or, better yet, going (or growing) from one state (of mind) to another. The Red Sea, of course, represents the delivering power of Jesus' blood.

In this edition, you will learn about the different types of boundaries that can be and should be set in the believer's life. You will also come to better understand your makeup as a human being, and why you may have dealt with some of the hardships that have plagued you over the course of your life. Also note that the color red represents hot; it is the color of fire that we mostly see. Red fire is about 600-800° Celsius; that is about 1112-1800° Fahrenheit.

TABLE OF CONTENTS

OUT OF BOUNDS

It all started in 2015. I'd just move to Georgia from Florida, and I was turning in for the night. I was finally where God wanted me to be, and this opened a portal that I'd never experienced. One night while lying down, I suddenly had a vision. It lasted for about a second or less; it left just as fast as it came. What did I see? A beautiful, royal and exquisite necklace. I remember being in awe and thinking about how pretty it had been. The lights were off in my room, so I thought about cutting them back on and writing down what I'd seen, but I was tired, so I went ahead and drifted off to sleep. I didn't think too much about it at first; that is, until I had another one a few days later. This time, it was another necklace. It was exquisite and like nothing I'd ever seen before. Once again, I was in the bed with my lights off, about to go to sleep. As always, I was fully awake. I hadn't started dozing off just yet. And once again, I decided not to cut the lights on and write down what I'd seen. I just planned to remember it and write it down later. This would happen several times before the visions suddenly stopped. I eventually moved out of the apartment I was living in and into a house an hour away. Of course, I would often think about those visions, and after I got into a church home and learned more about the prophetic, I realized why the visions had stopped. I hadn't respected them enough to write them down. I was acting entitled. I thought I could retrieve those ideas whenever I wanted to. Of course, I kept forgetting the detail in the necklaces, only remembering that they were beautiful, exquisite and they looked foreign. I repented and asked the Lord to start giving me those visions again.

In either late 2017 or early 2018, they started up again. And like always, they would leave as fast as they'd come, but this time, I was ready. I'd bought myself a journal and I'd started journaling what I saw. If I had a vision, I'd get over myself, cut the light back on and write down what I'd seen. Not long after this, the visions became even more interesting. I started having flashes of never-before-seen pieces of clothing. Now, I'm no fashion designer, so I wasn't sure why I was seeing clothes. I also had a vision of an extremely organized closet. There were color-coordinated beads in clear plastic containers, all set neatly in place on a few shelves. The room looked like a high-end department store. The walls were pure white and the room was orderly, colorful and breathtakingly beautiful. What was happening? Was I about to become a fashion designer or jewelry designer extraordinaire? Not exactly. The visions were not symbolic of what God wanted me to do; they symbolized access to strategies, invention ideas and the like; they represented access to revelation. The boundary that had once stood between me and this heavenly vault had now been removed. But back in 2015, because I didn't have a church home or anyone to help me understand what I had been experiencing, I'd completely disregarded what God was trying to show me. Consequently, I went through one of the most intense financial attacks that I'd ever undergone. The windows of Heaven were open, but I was still caught up in doing things my way.

By leaving Florida (my dream state) and coming to Georgia (a state I was never interested in), I'd obeyed God, and not just that, I was laying something else on my personal altar. We all have personal altars, and some of our altars are bloodier than others. Some people's altars are squeaky clean, while others have extremely bloody altars, meaning, they've sacrificed a lot for God's glory. And of course, the size of your sacrifice will determine the amount of blood it sheds. And by blood, I don't mean the blood that runs in our veins, I'm simply using symbolism. For example, I know women who've met the men they believed had been sent by God into their lives. They courted and everything seemed perfect at first; that is, until God told them to take a step back. Like most of us, they were grieved and they didn't want to believe that they were hearing from God. I've seen women pass this test, and I've seen women fail this test miserably. The ones who stepped away, grieved the relationship and allowed God to heal them almost always ended up with the guys they'd let go of. God sent those men back into their lives, they got married and they have the unions that most of us dream to have. Then again, the ones who refused to obey God often cut off everybody who echoed the voice of God in their lives (including their pastors); they surrounded themselves with enablers who said what they wanted to hear, and they either ended up getting dumped by their idols or, in some cases, they ended up marrying those guys. But

3

the ones who got married had unions that most of us pray to NEVER-EVER have. Their husbands are oftentimes narcissistic, controlling, abusive, religious, double-minded, unstable, promiscuous and half-crazy. When God told them to let those guys go, He wasn't trying to take the men away. He wanted to prepare both parties, deliver them from idolatry, fill their voids and heal some of their hearts' wounds. The women who obeyed God had extremely bloody altars, after all, letting go of someone you love is a major sacrifice. The women who disobeyed God often gave Him tithes, pigeon-dove sized offerings and they ran a few laps around their local sanctuaries during praise and worship. Their altars had a few drips of blood on them. Consequently, they ended up bleeding from the trauma of an ungodly relationship. You see, whenever you refuse to sacrifice anything for God's glory, that thing will cut and injure you. Please note that whatever you lay on your personal altar will oftentimes get back up and follow you. When this happens, you have to take it back to the altar and keep piercing it until you finally kill it. For example, let's say that God tells you to let go of your dream guy. You obey Him, and quite naturally, your former beau is heartbroken. You both reason within your hearts that it should be okay for you to be friends, after all, you are sisters and brothers in Christ. This would mean that your sacrifice is following you around—with your permission, of course. You'd have to fully and wholeheartedly let him go; this is the only way you'll properly grieve what you were building. This will allow God to set a new foundation in place. Otherwise, you'll keep building on a foundation that God has

4

rejected.

I'd started heading into a new region of thought, and the warfare that preceded me entering that new season wasn't just intense, it was almost unbearable. It was so bad that I questioned whether I'd truly heard God and whether the prophets and apostles who'd prophesied about God calling me to Georgia had been accurate. If God had truly called me to this place, why was I suddenly under such an immense attack? Wouldn't He protect me, if for no other reason than the fact that I was in His will? This line of reasoning clearly showed that I had humanized God. Not only that, but I was also transactional in my reasoning; this was a region of thought that God was in the process of delivering me from. You see, people who are transactional have a cause-and-effect ideology regarding God. They think that because they've done one thing, God is obligated to respond by giving them whatsoever it is that they want. This line of thinking often causes us to become angry with God because we feel like He didn't hold up His end of the deal when in truth obedience to God is a "reasonable service." In other words, it's the least we could do after all He's done for us. Obeying God does not obligate Him to giving us the desires of our hearts; it is our faith that compels Him to bless us with those desires. But before He gives us the desires of our hearts, He first gives us a new heart and a new mind. I'd obeyed Him and sacrificed my own comfort, so I expected the windows of Heaven to suddenly break open and pour out a blessing that I didn't have room enough to receive. And they did! But like most believers, I didn't understand what that looked like. I thought that when Heaven opened its windows, I would receive unexpected checks in the mail or one of my businesses would suddenly reach the million-dollar mark. I didn't realize that the word "pour" in the Bible means to send forth. God had sent me forth. In some of those visions, I was walking through what appeared to be a vault. I had windows of opportunity that I'd missed because I wasn't writing down what I'd seen, I wasn't pulling on those visions in prayer, and I'd let go of them far too easily. I now understand Matthew 11:12, which reads, "And from the days of John the Baptist until now the kingdom of heaven suffers violence, and the violent take it by force." I wasn't violent enough. Again, the Kingdom of God is within us! God was giving me a tour of His Kingdom, but I had to learn how to access it! In other words, I had potential that needed to be pulled out! This didn't just represent me pulling out my own potential, it represented God bringing me in contact with people who would pull on my potential as well. What's even more interesting is that the visions had never taken place while I was in Florida. This means that those prophetic words were true after all! God had truly called me to Georgia, and the attacks were the evidence of this fact! It meant that I was about to enter my personal promised land.

Let's look at some of the victories of Rahab. If you don't know the story, Rahab was a prostitute who'd helped two Israelite spies by hiding them in her house when they'd come to survey the land of Jericho. Most people would ask, "Why would a woman help a strange nation to take over her nation and kill her people? The answer may shock you—sometimes, God will allow you to be screwed over so many times (pun intended) to the point where you have absolutely no connection to the season that you're in or the people in that season! Men would show up at her door just to satisfy their sexual deviancy, and the women around town likely hated her. Like most of us, she probably had a rough childhood, and she'd questioned why things had been so difficult for her. But the answer showed up in her next season! God didn't want her to be committed to the season that she was in! Look at your life! Chances are, you've lived through some pretty hard seasons, and because of this, you had no loyalty to those seasons. It was easy for you to walk away because there was no incentive for you to stay where you were! For example, Conyers, Georgia was a place that I absolutely hated! At that time, I hadn't found my church tribe yet and I would often tell people that I wasn't willing to travel anymore than twenty minutes to go to church. This was because I feared Georgia's traffic. The thought of traveling 45 minutes one way was a nightmare for me. Unbeknownst to me, however, the church God had picked for me was about an hour away from where I was living. Hearing my confession, God allowed the brook to dry up where I was at so that I could move closer to the church He'd picked for me.

One day, a woman I knew started talking about a church that was maybe thirty to forty minutes away from where I was living at the time. She wanted to take me and a few other people there that following Friday because that particular church had a prophetic event every Friday night. Mind you, I was still under an immense spiritual attack and I was beyond desperate for a Word from God. I agreed to go, and that Thursday night, I found myself on my knees pleading with God. "I need a Word from you," I cried. "This is too much for me! Please speak with me tomorrow night!" The next night, we went to the event, but we got there late, so we weren't able to sign up to get a meeting with a team of prophets. While I was disappointed and devastated, I had no choice but to believe that God would find a way to speak to me. I remember one of the ushers having me and the people I'd come with to move to the front row, even though we had arrived late. They preached and taught, and before the service ended, the speaker announced that they were going to release a few prophets on the floor, and if they had a word for anyone, they would come and share that word. While she was making this announcement, one of the prophets who was standing behind her looked at me. She didn't blink or turn her head, she just stared at me intently. I smiled inwardly because I knew what that meant—she had a word for me! God had answered my prayer! When it was her turn to prophesy, she grabbed the mic and made her way back to the front of the church. "Can you please stand?" she asked me. I obliged, of course. She then asked me to lift my hands. She told me that I had been under a very intense spiritual attack. As she spoke, she gestured with her arms. She said, "I see Satan throwing dart after dart at you!" But this wasn't the shocker; what she said next got my attention. She told me that God was about to remove some people from my life because they meant me no good. I don't know why hearing this excited me. I felt stuck, overwhelmed and defeated, but after receiving that prophetic word, I felt a huge sense of relief. I had been questioning everything—my move, my associations and my faith! This, at least, seemed to give me a little direction. She also prophesied that she saw music all around me. "I see music coming out of you; it's all around you!" she said excitedly. Nevertheless, I don't have a pleasant singing voice. No one in their right mind would hand me a mic and ask me to sing. Nevertheless, I didn't question the words that she was releasing. I knew that somehow, some way and someday everything she was speaking would come to pass. And this didn't take long at all! By the time the lease on my apartment started coming to an end, I literally didn't have a friend left in Conyers. And get this, I hadn't removed anyone from my life. I hadn't yelled at anyone, accused anyone of anything, spoke ill of anyone—nothing! I simply obeyed God and loved the people in my life, and whenever they acted out, I held my peace because I didn't want to sabotage the move of God. I was eerily silent, and before long, I was all alone. That season had completely dried up. Frustrated and desperate to move, I applied for a bunch of houses online, determined to never live in an apartment again. One day, I received an email that I had been approved for the house I'm in now. It was an hour away from Conyers and I couldn't wait to check the place out. When I pulled into the driveway to check the house out, I remember feeling emotional and grateful. A year later, a friend of mine came into town from California and asked me to meet her at one of two churches. She texted me the options, and I chose the church I'm in today. I felt God when I opened their website; that's when I started shouting to her, "This is it! This is where God has called me to!" What's amazing is, my house is exactly twenty minutes away from my church. Again, God heard my confession and He perfectly positioned me so that I could get in place.

Why did I share that story? To make a point, of course. Rahab likely didn't have a friend in sight; she had no connections or loyalty to her people because they had been mistreating her. She was likely frustrated and tired of those late-night knocks and the judgmental stares. The same was true for me. While I wasn't having sex with anyone, the season I was in had become so frustratingly tense that I simply could not commit to it or the people in it. My season or the region of thought I was in had completely dried up. And anytime you're in a region that no longer serves you, the enemy will attack you without mercy. This is because in that moment, you are literally outside the will of God! Think about a kingdom that's being surrounded by potential attackers. That city has walls and it has an army, but if someone goes outside that city's walls, they are free-game. The attackers will capture, torture or kill them. This is what it looks like to be outside the walls of God or, better yet, outside the will of God. Think about that the next time you find yourself under an attack that won't seem to lift. Either you are in a season that God has told you to come out of or you're about to enter your personal promised land. Let's look at Joshua's victories; these are the victories that preceded him entering the Promised Land.

Joshua 7:12-24: And these are the kings of the country which Joshua and the children of Israel smote on this side Jordan on the west, from Baalgad in the valley of Lebanon even unto the mount Halak, that goeth up to Seir; which Joshua gave unto the tribes of Israel for a possession according to their divisions; In the mountains, and in the valleys, and in the plains, and in the springs, and in the wilderness, and in the south country; the Hittites, the Amorites, and the Canaanites, the Perizzites, the Hivites, and the Jebusites: The king of Jericho, one; the king of Ai, which is beside Bethel, one; The king of Jerusalem, one; the king of Hebron, one; The king of Jarmuth, one; the king of Lachish, one; The king of Eglon, one; the king of Gezer, one; The king of Debir, one; the king of Geder, one; The king of Hormah, one; the king of Arad, one; The king of Libnah, one; the king of Adullam, one; The king of Makkedah, one; the king of Bethel, one; The king of Tappuah, one; the king of Hepher, one; The king of Aphek, one; the king of Lasharon, one; The king of Madon, one; the king of Hazor, one; The king of Shimronmeron, one; the king of Achshaph, one; The king of Taanach, one; the king of Megiddo, one; The king of Kedesh, one; the king of Jokneam of Carmel, one; The king of Dor in the coast of Dor, one; the king of the nations of Gilgal, one; The king of Tirzah, one: all the kings thirty and one.

In total, Joshua had to fight 13 wars before he entered the Promised Land. When we are pursuing our personal promised lands, we often neglect to take into account the amount of warfare that we will face before entering those regions of thought. Please understand that you're not entering a reality; you are creating one. In other words, you won't step into a season where everything is handed to you. Instead, God gives us all the ingredients to create the realities we want. Like God had done with Moses, He gave me a preview of what I could possess, but I wasn't going to just walk in and possess the promise without any resistance. Anytime you are entering a region of thought, you have to overcome the strongmen of that region. In other words, the Kingdom of Heaven suffers violence, and the violent takes it by force! The average believer gives up the minute they are faced with opposition, especially when the enemy starts threatening or attacking their relationships. Every ungodly or outdated relationship serves as a leash of sorts. The soul tie wraps itself around the people who God is trying to promote, pulling them back into those seasons. This is when they face the Big U; that is, the big ultimatum. Either they can stay as they are and keep the folks they love and honor the most or they could lose it all and start a journey towards a new reality. The average Christian is not willing to pay the price associated with upgrade; we all ask for promotion, but most of us don't understand what this entails. So, in our religious ignorance, we sit and wait for God to move, often justifying our procrastination and our lack of movement with, "What God has for me is for me" or "I'm waiting on God. It's all in

His timing." Consequently, we find ourselves being passive participants in our own deliverance. In other words, we end up becoming masterminds of the regions of thought we're in. Again, a person who masterminds a region of thought is a manipulative character! And get this—whenever we're stuck in a season, we try to manipulate God into blessing us! We jump, shout, run laps around the church, dance, fall out and lift our hands, all the while, rebelling against God in our personal lives. That's all religiousness is if you think about it! It's attempting to manipulate God with works and performances, rather than adjusting our heart's posture. It's our way of trying to get God to bring our personal promised lands to us, rather than us doing the hard work of studying to show ourselves approved for those seasons. Many of us like to have things handed to us, but when we're tested with warfare, we often discover that we are nowhere near ready for an upgrade, even though we don't want to admit this.

Before God promoted me to my next season, I had to set a LOT of boundaries, not just for others, but for myself. Once I set and enforced those boundaries, He took me past a limitation—but this boundary wasn't one that I'd cross and end up bound. No, He lifted the limits; He gave me access to revelation and many of the treasures of the Kingdom of God, but unfortunately, there were some people who couldn't come along with me. I learned that while we may love the folks in our lives and have many plans for them, if God can't trust them to go where we're headed, chances are, they are temporary fixtures. This doesn't mean that they're bad people. Honestly, we have to get delivered from the notion that everyone who has graduated or was demoted out of our lives is a bad person. Sometimes, they are good people who have completed their assignments in our lives, and without them, we wouldn't be where are are today. Here's a pattern that you'll see whenever someone's season is up in your life.

- **They'll start dominating the conversations.** In other words, they'll do 80 percent or more of the talking, and if you try to cut in, they'll normally get off the phone, put you on hold or start yelling at their children in the background. For example, while you're talking, you may hear your friend suddenly say to her daughter, "Go and bring me your backpack. What did your teacher say about your science project?" This is a tool or a wile designed to help them regain control of the conversation. So, if you say, "Huh?" or "Are you speaking to me?" they will normally counter with, "No, I was talking to Willow. She had a science project to turn in today. She made a volcano, and she said the teacher loved it. That's why I love her teacher. She's always uplifting Willow, unlike her former teacher. Oh wait, did I tell you what happened to me today?" This is typically a manifestation of fear-based control. It normally happens when a person realizes that the season of that relationship is coming to an end or has already ended.

- **Some will indirectly insist on being the caller.** In other words, they won't answer the majority of your calls. They have to be the ones doing most of the calling, so whenever you call them, they will send you to voicemail. You calling them indicates to them that you want to talk, and at this stage in your relationship with them, they are not willing to spend a lot of time listening. They have to be the ones doing the majority of the talking, so they'll often ignore your calls.

- **Others will stop calling you, insisting on you being the caller**, and if you don't call, they'll get offended and say things like, "I guess you're too important to call people these days" or "Hey stranger." People who are dealing with suspicion typically do this. Because they've been talking about you to others, they assume that you're doing the same. In some cases, they worry that the folks they've been slandering you to may have reached out to you and told you what they've said. So, out of fear, they will often wait for you to call them or, in some cases, this is just their way of seeing if you're mad at them.

- **If you miss one of their calls, you can sense their offense**, even if it's not verbally communicated. It's passively communicated by their refusal to answer your calls whenever you attempt to call them back; yes, even if you call them three seconds after you've missed their calls! Sometimes, this "punishment" can last for days or weeks.

- **They will talk nonstop about the past**, and if you speak futuristically, they'll normally power down those conversations by saying something negative, by changing the subject or by getting off the phone with you. For example, if you say, "I'm so excited! God finally released me to write the book I told you about," they may respond with, "That's good. But make sure you don't be talking in circles in that book. You're good for that!" or "That's good. Congratulations. Well girl, let me get off this phone. I have to help Willow with her school project."

- **You feel drained or guilty after speaking with them.** This is because they will often engage you in conversations that you don't want to have. They'll talk negatively about everything and everyone, and they'll try to provoke you to add your own negative input into the dialogue. If you do, they will strategically end the conversation on your negative note. In many cases, you may say something that you shouldn't have said, with the intent of turning the conversation into a positive one. For example, they may say, "Dana has been really testing me lately! Ever since she got married, she keeps talking nonstop about her husband and all these countries they have traveled to! Yesterday, she called me talking about her trip to Venezuela. I'm happy for her and all, but I feel like she's just rubbing it in my face to make me jealous! Why would I be jealous of her? Her husband isn't even cute!" To this, you may say, "Yeah, Dana has always been a chatty person, and she talks a lot about her traveling whenever she calls me. It can be annoying at times because I can't relate to it, plus, when she gets excited, her already high-pitched voice gets even more annoying, but ..." And from there, your friend will cut in and say, "Hold on! Hey, let me call you back!" Now, you feel guilty because you were trying to shift the conversation. You were about to say something positive about Dana, but you didn't get a chance to. The conversation ended on a negative note, and now, you feel like you were gossiping about Dana when, in truth, you were simply trying to relate to your friend before defending Dana. This is what the Bible refers to as being "ensnared by the words of your mouth." Some conversations are nothing but traps.

- **They start indirectly threatening you.** This is the Big U or ultimatum. For example, your friend may say, "I called Dana yesterday, and once again, she didn't answer my call. And guess what? I'm not calling her back. She'll need me before I need her. I was there for her when that crazy husband of hers split her lip and pulled her hair out. I was there for her when her own daddy had nothing to do with her. And now, she's acting funny, but that's okay. I always tell people that they'll need me before I'll need them. That's why you don't burn bridges with folks." This message isn't about Dana at all! It's an indirect threat to you! It's her way of saying that if you don't straighten up or you continue doing whatever it is that you're doing, she's going to distance herself from you AND you will regret what you've done the minute you find yourself in a storm without her. These indirect threats normally

17

come when you haven't responded favorably to all of their other tricks and gimmicks.

Of course, the list goes on, but these are all tools of manipulation, and manipulation is one of the many flavors of witchcraft. Remember, witchcraft is a fruit of the flesh that can and oftentimes does become demonic. It simply means that the person has mastered a region of thought and that person may have even mastered us! They know what buttons to press, how hard to press them and how long to press them to get the responses they want out of us. When they resort to these wiles, God will often remove them from our lives because they are fighting against the changes He's making to our lives. This is partly or mostly because they identify us by our pasts and have trouble accepting our futures. They want us to remain the same. Some people will embrace and even celebrate those changes, even if it means that the two of you won't be close friends anymore, and God will often allow them to remain connected to you. But anyone who fights against your evolution is the very definition of an enemy! One of the signs or symptoms that someone's time is up in your life is when you feel drained every time you speak with that person. Truth be told, many of the relationships that end are not because God wants that person out of our lives; sometimes, He simply wants to transition those relationships. For example, someone who was once your best friend may suddenly become a distant friend, but that person may not be willing to accept his or her new role, and this is understandable. Howbeit, you cannot continue to serve in an outdated role. It's a big adjustment to make, and some people are not willing to make it. If they refuse to transition into a new role, God then requires you to sacrifice those relationships. In other words, your altar has to get a little bloodier before you exit that season. And to sacrifice a relationship, you don't necessarily have to call people and tell them that their seasons are up in your life. You simply need to change! Amos 3:3 says, "Can two walk together, except they be agreed?" In other words, it's time to change your agreements by changing your mind! So, if your friend is a gossiper and you normally listen to her gossip, stop it! Buy a few books about gossip and slander, read those books, recommit your ears to God and communicate your new boundaries to your friend. Keep creating and enforcing boundaries to keep evil out of your communications with her and anyone in your life. This will essentially evict her because she'll realize that she has nothing to talk to you about; she has nothing in common with you! She'll then find herself a new friend or rekindle a friendship that she once let go of, and she will call you less and less. When she does call you, she'll test you to see if you're still holding onto your new boundaries. She'll slip a little gossip in, and this is where you have to stop her! One effective way to do this is to insist on praying for the person that she wants to gossip about. This causes gossipers to feel a level of humiliation, and again, she'll go a few weeks or months without calling you. She'll continue doing this until she realizes that you're not going to let up. You are truly a new creature in Christ!

SPIRITUAL STRANGULATION: THE PYTHON SPIRIT

What happens if you don't let go of a relationship that God is calling you out of? What happens if you refuse to change your mind? In 2 Corinthians 6:14, Apostle Paul uses a phrase that we have all become familiar with, and that phrase is "unequally yoked." The scripture reads, "Be ye not unequally yoked together with unbelievers: for what fellowship hath righteousness with unrighteousness? And what communion hath light with darkness?" What is a yoke? Google's online dictionary defines it this way, "A wooden crosspiece that is fastened over the necks of two animals and attached to the plow or cart that they are to pull."

The neck of a person or an animal connects its head (authority) with its body (members). This is what allows the brain (thinker) to attach to those who are set to carry out the mission. In other words, you have purpose, even if no one has ever communicated this to you. Nevertheless, you cannot and will not fulfill that purpose when you are attached to the wrong people. And by unbelievers, this isn't just referencing unsaved people; this scripture is also dealing with people who live in the dark as it relates to you. They are blinded by God to your purpose and potential; this is because if they saw what God was planning to do to, for and through you, they would go out of their way to sabotage His plans! This would put them in direct danger because no one can wrestle against God and win! They are unbelievers because they don't believe you are anointed, nor do they believe that God can or will use you at the capacity that He wants to use you at. They feel like they are more anointed than you or they are more deserving of God's favor than you. So, a soul tie with someone like this will begin to harden and become a yoke. It will keep you stuck to a pattern, a cycle and a region of thought, and it will drive away the people who God wants to connect you with. When a soul tie becomes a yoke, it begins to strangle your purpose, your assignment and your potential. When a person begins to operate in this capacity, chances are, they have a python spirit or they are about to pick one up!

What is a python spirit? It is one of the many spirits that fall under the category of a constrictor or constricting spirit; it's similar to the python snake because it wraps itself around a person and begins to squeeze that individual, causing him or her to feel lethargic, depressed, defeated, etc. Sound familiar? Another constrictor is the spirit of fear. What typically happens is, whenever you're about to exit a season or a region of thought, you will often begin to experience the fear of the unknown. All the same, seeing the changes that God is making to your life, any person whose season in your life is coming to an end will oftentimes experience the fear of losing you. Now, don't confuse this fear with love. It's the fear of change, fear of watching you accomplish something outside of their influence, fear of being alone, etc. Another constrictor that you'll come across in this network is jealousy. One of the most dangerous people to have in your life is someone who deals with entitlement and jealousy—someone who wholeheartedly, passionately and genuinely believes that they deserve God's favor more than you! This is why the Bible says that jealousy is as cruel as the grave! The grave is constricting; it's a pit where no activity takes place, other than the decomposition and deterioration of your assignment. And finally, jealousy will often pair up with another constrictor, and that is sabotage! This particular spirit will work tirelessly to destroy any opportunity of growth and ascension that it sees on the horizon for you. These constrictors will work together with python to squeeze the life out of your purpose. Since python is the head or the strongman in this particular network, let's look at some of its characteristics.

Characteristics of the Python Spirit
1 **It requires a lot of affirmation.** People who have this spirit have to be affirmed and reaffirmed time and time again. For example, you may find yourself always trying to explain your actions or words so that they won't feel rejected or offended. If you are a woman who has female friends, it starts to feel odd when you're having to explain yourself in the same manner that you would do with an insecure man if you were in a relationship. For example, you may find yourself saying things like— "Like I told her, me and her are friends, but you're my best friend. I trust you more than

I trust anyone else!" This conversation indicates that you sense her insecurities regarding the other person, and you don't just sense those insecurities, but she is somehow communicating them. So, you'll spend a lot of time pacifying her voids and her fears.

2	**It is an attention-seeking spirit.** Someone who has this spirit will demand or require a lot of your time and attention. They love to be the center of attention anywhere they go!
3	**It uses flattery as bait.** Someone who has this spirit will often flatter you, making it difficult for you to detect their jealousy and every other vile thing that's in their heart for you.
4	**It wants to be the most important fixture in your life.** Someone who has this spirit will often display signs of jealousy whenever you are sharing your time and attention with another person, especially if you are close to that person or if that person is slowly becoming a close friend or important fixture in your life.
5	**It employs the use of false prophecy.** It is a spirit of divination that likes to take some truths, pepper them with lies and flattery, and serve them to you so that your relationship with that person will appear to be God-approved.
6	**It is a transactional spirit.** In other words, people who have this spirit will give you time, money, compliments or whatever they can give you to gain

your trust. But nothing that they give to you is free! It all has motive attached to it.

7	**It employs the use of fear, jealousy and whatever tools it can find to keep you under its control.** Someone who has this spirit will play a lot of mind-games, for example, your friend may start posting subliminal messages on Facebook that are designed to scare you back into submission. She may say, "It's funny how some folks call you their friend, but they don't know that you know how they really feel about you! The Lord is a revealer of hearts! That's okay! Let them keep pretending and just act like you don't know that they are snakes!" A post like this will almost always incite fear and curiosity because your first thought is, "Did I do or say something that may have offended her?"

Acts 16:16-24 tells the story of a young woman who was bound by the python spirit. It reads, "And it came to pass, as we went to prayer, a certain damsel possessed with a spirit of divination met us, which brought her masters much gain by soothsaying: The same followed Paul and us, and cried, saying, These men are the servants of the most high God, which shew unto us the way of salvation. And this did she many days. But Paul, being grieved, turned and said to the spirit, I command thee in the name of Jesus Christ to come out of her. And he came out the same hour. And when her masters saw that the hope of their gains was gone, they caught Paul and Silas, and drew them into the marketplace

unto the rulers, And brought them to the magistrates, saying, These men, being Jews, do exceedingly trouble our city, And teach customs, which are not lawful for us to receive, neither to observe, being Romans. And the multitude rose up together against them: and the magistrates rent off their clothes, and commanded to beat them. And when they had laid many stripes upon them, they cast them into prison, charging the jailer to keep them safely: Who, having received such a charge, thrust them into the inner prison, and made their feet fast in the stocks."

Let's extract a few facts from this passage.

Facts	Revelation
It manifested when the men went into prayer.	The python spirit hates prayer and worship! It was trying to stop the men from praying, and it used the tool of flattery in an attempt to keep them from seeing its agenda.
The woman bound by it was a slave.	Bound people bind people. Someone who has this spirit is a slave of a season or a region of thought.
She helped her masters to make a living through her soothsaying.	It is a spirit of false prophecy! It will often gain your trust by giving you some truths that you want, and the moment you stop guarding your heart, it will then begin to inject lies and fear into your heart. This is the moment right before

Facts	Revelation
	constriction takes place!
It followed Apostle Paul and Silas.	Someone with this spirit is normally an avid follower of true men and women of God. But make no mistake about it, their followship is not a sign of loyalty to the people or the person they are following. It is a sign of their loyalty to destroying that individual or movement.
It declared the truth about the men, saying they were men of God who would lead them to salvation.	This is a spirit that loves to use flattery to gain trust. Someone with this spirit will say some of the nicest things to and about you, but the same way they spoke good of you, they will eventually turn around and speak evil of you. These are the people who go live on social media to "expose" their pastors after they've been offended. When the video comes on, you will likely find them wearing a tallit or playing something super spiritual. They will cry in the video and will appear very humble, but make no mistake about it—they are predators masquerading as prey!
The men were beaten and jailed for casting out this spirit.	Anytime you come against the python spirit, you can expect the people in that bound person's life to react and respond. This is because they've been

Facts	Revelation
	benefiting off that person somehow.

Why did Paul, Silas and the other men come across this spirit? Because they were:

1. In a certain region where this spirit was accepted.
2. Because they were advancing the Kingdom of God.

Remember this; rehearse it in your mind—anyone who has mastered a particular region of thought is a manipulator! Manipulation and rebellion are both fruits or flavors of witchcraft! So, a person who is holding you hostage to a region of thought using any of the aforementioned constrictors is a person who is either being used by the python spirit or someone who is unknowingly auditioning to be used by this spirit! There are levels to witchcraft, just as there are ranks of spirits. People ascend into witchcraft through rebellion; it normally starts off as low-level witchcraft, for example, your friend may begin gossiping about you. Gossip is one of the many cords of witchcraft! Gossip pairs with sabotage to keep you from advancing. Please note that we are multidimensional creatures, and there are many states to us. Satan advances through any of the following states:

- Your mental state
- Your physical state
- Your religious state
- Your parental state
- Your familial state

- Your platonic state
- Your romantic state
- Your sexual state
- Your career state
- Your financial state

In this particular case, he's likely in your platonic state; he entered there through your friendship. And he may have attacked your romantic state from there. Your friend may have given you a lot of bad advice. It will go into every state that it can enter, and then, begin its constriction. And it doesn't just use friends, it'll use any door that it finds open! Every person in your life is a door! If a person does not guard his or her heart, that person is an open door! And remember, Satan will never pass by an open door unless you're in the will of God, which means, he's not allowed in the room! Python will use your career, your family, your significant or insignificant other or any threshold it can cross to keep you in a specific region of thought! One of its favorite tools is false loyalty. In this, the people around you who are bound by this spirit will make you feel obligated to pacifying their fears, rejection or their unwillingness to be alone.

As you journey from season to season, you will come across a lot of people, all of whom are within the confines of their own seasons. Remember this, if you pair winter with summer, a storm is inevitable. In other words, don't get mad when you're not invited into a circle! Some circles are nothing but a bunch of tangled up soul ties that are now serving as leashes, and believe me when I say that people have a way of making bondage look inviting! This is why I don't bother trying to fit in. I often say this—stop trying to fit in before you mess around and succeed! Again, most cliques only have openings for certain roles. If the only roles that are open within a particular circle is the role of a clown and the role of a security guard, you can mess around and get drafted into one of those roles. This is how people "lose themselves." The soul is impressionable; remember that. So, if the opening requires you to be square, your soul will eventually take on that shape. You'll become what they want at the detriment of your identity and assignment. Additionally, please note that people can and oftentimes do elevate to a region of thought, and then end up getting bound in that region. This is normally because they refuse to allow God to grow and change them. Their altars are cold; there is no activity or blood on those altars! And when you refuse to give God anything He requires or requests from you, that thing or that person will become an idol in your life. This includes your friends, and while you may not physically worship them, you are sacrificing your future for them, and this is an act of worship. But again, there are people who have gotten stuck in regions of thought, and they have mastered those regions of thought! These are the people Satan will use to constrict you whenever you enter that season! They will flatter you, invite you into their circles and then begin to distract you since these people need a lot of attention. Again, they are oftentimes in partnership with the python spirit; this is why they do not and cannot prosper! Isaiah 54:17 says, "No weapon that is formed against thee shall prosper; and every tongue that shall rise against thee in judgment thou shalt condemn. This is the heritage of the servants of the LORD, and their righteousness is of me, saith the LORD." They are weapons! This scripture isn't talking about bullets and knives; it's talking about people! And it's not just saying that they won't succeed in their evil plans, it's literally saying that because of their wicked hearts, their rebellious ways and their partnership with the enemy, prosperity will avoid them! This is why they can't seem to escape a certain income bracket; this is why they fill out a lot of applications, but nobody calls them back! The same python spirit that they are using to hold and constrict you has wrapped itself around their potential and is squeezing the life out of it! It's important for you to note that your success is found in your obedience, and by success, I'm not just talking about monetary gain. Money is just one of the many fruits of success; it's not the entire tree. Success is wholeness; it is lacking nothing in any area or state of your life! The point is, there are boundaries that we have to cross, there are boundaries that we are not supposed to cross, and then there are seasons that expire. And when a season of your life expires, but you don't move out of it, you will end up on the wrong side of a boundary, and consequently, you can end up stuck.

TRAUMA: SATAN'S FAVORITE STENCIL

Below, you'll find a few definitions of trauma.

Definition	Source
An emotional response to a terrible event like an accident, rape or natural disaster. Immediately after the event, shock and denial are typical. Longer term reactions include unpredictable emotions, flashbacks, strained relationships and even physical symptoms like headaches or nausea. While these feelings are normal, some people have difficulty moving on with their lives. Psychologists can help these individuals find constructive ways of managing their emotions.	American Psychological Association
a disordered psychic or behavioral state resulting from severe mental or emotional stress or physical injury	Merriam Webster
a deeply distressing or disturbing experience.	Oxford Languages

There are three types or levels of trauma. The following was taken from Early Childhood Mental Health:
Listed below are the different types of trauma:

Trauma Types	Definitions
Acute	Results from exposure to a single overwhelming event/experiences (car accident, natural disaster, single event of abuse or assault, sudden loss or witnessing violence).
Repetitive	Results from exposure to multiple, chronic and/or prolonged overwhelming traumatic events. (i.e., receiving regular treatment for an illness).
Complex	Results from multiple, chronic and prolonged overwhelming traumatic events/experiences which are compromising and most often within the context of an interpersonal relationship. (i.e., family violence).
Developmental	Results from early onset exposure to ongoing or repetitive trauma (as infant, children or youth) includes neglect, abandonment, physical abuse or assault, sexual abuse or assault, emotional abuse witnessing violence or death, and/or coercion or betrayal.

Trauma Types	Definitions
	This often occurs within the child's care giving system and interferes with healthy attachment and development.
Vicarious	Creates a change in the service provider resulting from empathetic engagement with a client's/patient's traumatic background. It occurs when an individual who was not an immediate witness to the trauma absorbs and integrates disturbing aspects of the traumatic experience into his or her own functioning.
Historical	Historical trauma is a cumulative emotional and psychological wounding over the lifespan and across generations emanating from massive group trauma. Examples of historical trauma include genocide, colonialism (i.e., residential schools), slavery and war.
Intergenerational	Intergenerational trauma describes the psychological or emotional effects that can be experienced by people who live with people who have experienced trauma. Coping and adaptation patterns developed in response to trauma can be passed

Trauma Types	Definitions
	from one generation to the next.

(Source: Your Experience Matters/Types of Trauma/IWK Healthcare)

Trauma is a stencil designed to shape or mold you into what Satan has decided that he wants you to be. Most believers are completely ignorant of the enemy's devices, and because of this, we tend to be emotional while the enemy is being strategic. Many of the people who are housed in mental institutions are gifted or called by God, but they have a long history of trauma. Trauma, coupled with a lack of information or an overflow of knowledge with no understanding, is a recipe for insanity. Romans 11:29 reads, "For the gifts and calling of God are without repentance." In other words, you don't have to be saved to be gifted! You don't have to be in the will of God to be called! But you do have to be in the will of God to truly answer that call! Think about systemic and systematic racism. Please note that systemic refers to something that has been weaved into a system, whereas, the word systematic describes the methodical process that something is accomplished. As we all know (regardless of our racial backgrounds), there were systems put in place to halt the progression of African Americans and Indian-Americans. Let's look at some of these laws.

Racist Laws	Source
Between 1740 and 1834 Alabama, Georgia, Louisiana, Mississippi, North and South Carolina, and Virginia all passed anti-literacy laws. South Carolina prohibited teaching slaves to read and write, punishable by a fine of 100 pounds and six months in prison, via an amendment to its 1739 Negro Act.	Wikipedia
• 1819, Missouri: Prohibited assembling or teaching slaves to read or write. • 1829, Georgia: Prohibited teaching blacks to read, punished by fine and imprisonment. • 1832, Alabama and Virginia: Prohibited whites from teaching blacks to read or write, punished by fines and floggings. • 1833, Georgia: Prohibited blacks from working in reading or writing jobs (via an employment law), and prohibited teaching blacks, punished by fines and whippings (via an anti-literacy law). • 1847, Missouri: Prohibited teaching blacks to read or write.	Wikipedia
Excerpt from South Carolina Act of 1740: Whereas, the having slaves taught to write, or suffering them to be employed in writing, may be attended with great inconveniences; Be it enacted, that all and every person and	Thirteen/Media With Impact/The Slave Experience)

37

Racist Laws	Source
persons whatsoever, who shall hereafter teach or cause any slave or slaves to be taught to write, or shall use or employ any slave as a scribe, in any manner of writing whatsoever, hereafter taught to write, every such person or persons shall, for every such offense, forfeit the sum of one hundred pounds, current money.	
Excerpt from Virginia Revised Code of 1819: That all meetings or assemblages of slaves, or free Negroes or mulattoes mixing and associating with such slaves at any meeting-house or houses in the night; or at any SCHOOL OR SCHOOLS for teaching them READING OR WRITING, either in the day or night, under whatsoever pretext, shall be deemed and considered an UNLAWFUL ASSEMBLY; and any justice of a county, wherein such assemblage shall be, either from his own knowledge or the information of others, of such unlawful assemblage may issue his warrant, directed to any sworn officer or officers, authorizing him or them to enter the house or houses where such unlawful assemblages maybe for the purpose of apprehending or dispersing such slaves, and to inflict corporal punishment on the offender or offenders, at the discretion of any	Thirteen/Media With Impact/The Slave Experience)

Racist Laws	Source
justice of the peace, not exceeding twenty lashes.	

Why were Blacks prohibited from learning? Again, this is both systemic racism and systematic racism. It was designed to stop African Americans from becoming independent of White Americans' influence. It was a form of slavery within itself. Racists had an idea regarding how they wanted Blacks to be. Many wanted Blacks to remain as slaves, especially in the South. This was an example of a generational curse on their parts. Many wanted Blacks to be free, but didn't want them to have the same rights, education and opportunities as Whites. This was all due to a White supremacy mindset. Consequently, they hurt and traumatized Blacks time and time again, trying to get us to, as some used to say "stay in a Negro's place." But what was a Negro's place? It was whatever belief the oppressing party had in regards to Blacks. If a man believed that Blacks should live in ghettos, be second-class citizens and allow themselves to be oppressed, raped, used and abused by Whites, this is what he meant. Pain was the stencil that he used to accomplish this. Again, this is a perfect example of how Satan perverts and breaks people until they fit into the mold he has created for them.

Every African American has been touched by racism, if not personally, we've been touched by it generationally. This is called indirect trauma. The racist White guy in the 1910's has still managed to affect our lives, even if we were born in the 1990's. This is because the trauma suffered through our grandparents, great-grandparents and great-great grandparents somehow managed to reach across the hands of time to alter our thinking as well. For example, if our great-great grandparents witnessed lynchings, were raped, endured harassment and were oppressed, they ended up traumatized. Some of them were severely traumatized! They lived with fear, anger, guilt, shame and every other spirit that comes after oppressed people. They were traumatized when they raised our great-grandparents, so they traumatized their children (our grandparents) who, in turn, traumatized their children (our parents) who, in turn, traumatized us. And now that we have children, we may have traumatized them as well. This cycle perpetuates itself until someone decides to risk it all to break it. It continues to play out until someone stops using their trauma as an excuse to remain average or to live a life of defeat. It takes a person who's willing to offend the majority, if not the entirety of his or her family by going against familial norms. For example, if the matriarch of the family is a traumatized, narcissistic great-aunt who uses her money, influence and emotions to get what she wants, someone has to be willing to offend her. Someone has to be willing to step back over the boundary that surrounds their authenticity and their identities and stake a claim to their God-given authority. And by offending her, they have to be willing to deal with the flying monkeys that are in their family; these are the family members who will come to defend the great-aunt and her policies. What is a flying monkey?

"Flying monkeys can be anyone who believes the narcissist's fake persona including the narcissist's spouse, child, friend, sibling or cousin. According to popular psychology author Angela Atkinson, flying monkeys are usually unwittingly manipulated people who believe the smears about the victim although they may be another narcissist working in tandem. According to narcissistic personality disorder (NPD) author Sam Vaknin, and other writers, proxy abusers can come from a number of sources:

- the abuser's associates
- the victim's associates—manipulated to side with the abuser
- authority and institutional figures—manipulated to side with the abuser.

The flying monkey does the narcissist's bidding to inflict additional torment on the target. This may consist of spying, spreading gossip, threatening, painting the narcissist as the victim (victim playing) and the target as the perpetrator (victim blaming). Despite this, the narcissist does not hesitate to make flying monkeys his or her scapegoats when and if needed.

The flying monkeys may make it seem like the narcissist is not really involved, and they likely have no idea that they are being used. Multiple flying monkeys act as a mobbing force against a victim." (Source: Wikipedia.com)

Again, someone in that family has to offend and come against the norm; they not only have to be cognizant of the price they'll likely pay for not allowing themselves to be further controlled or traumatized, they have to be willing to pay that price, even if it means that the entirety of their family decides to disown them. The goal is for the individual to heal and then to lead his or her family to healing. In other words, the individual must be willing to confront his or her own demons, oftentimes alone; this way, he or she can be a curse-breaker in his or her family. Sadly enough, not many people are willing to take on this role. Many will volunteer, but most will go and resubmit to the policies of their great-aunt, not realizing that she is the product of systemic and systematic racism. She's found a way to function in her dysfunction. Believe it or not, she is a slave who is still bound by her great-grandparents' masters. But unlike the slaves that worked in the field, she has found a way to make the system work for her, however, in order for her to remain in the comforts of her insanity, she has to monitor, harass and point out any family members who may be out of place. Again, she is the product of trauma; this is why you cannot continue to allow yourself to be controlled, manipulated and bullied by her. Someone has to come and set the captives free. This person is called a curse-breaker.

For African Americans, many of our parents, especially those of us from the South, raised us while suffering from PTSD (Post Traumatic Stress Syndrome). Again, this trauma had been brought on by a history of racism, oppression, abuse, fear-tactics and ignorance. Systemic racism and oppression ensured that they would not get the information needed to change their lives by changing their minds. In other words, they had been falling down the bottomless pit for hundreds, if not thousands of years, and we were born into those falls. And like them, we did not respect boundaries, so we rebelled against them. Consequently, we got hurt time and time again, not realizing that Satan was working through that trauma to attack our minds all the more, after all, the battleground is in the mind. And for many of us, we can now look back and truly say that we should've been crazy, but it was only the grace of God that kept us! But this brings about the question—why would God keep some people, but allow others to lose their minds? First and foremost, people don't truly lose their minds; the enemy simply advanced on their mental states until they were in captivity in just about every arena of thought. He used a personalized stencil to get them into the mental shape he wanted them in. This stencil is more like a recipe; it is oftentimes prolonged abuse, repeated rejections and a lack of information. At the same time, the word "kept" in this context doesn't necessarily mean that God stored our minds in a vault and told the enemy that he could not touch it. Remember that God drew a standard around Job's life, BUT this standard was one-sided! It kept the enemy from taking Job's life, but it did not stop Job from taking his own life! He clearly became suicidal; he was definitely on the brink of insanity, but as long as he stayed in the will of God, his mind was protected. Howbeit, his wife eventually became straitjacket worthy. Job 2:9

43

states, "Then said his wife unto him, Dost thou still retain thine integrity? Curse God, and die." Of course, Job refused her offer and rebuked her. His response is recorded in Job 2:10, which reads, "But he said unto her, Thou speakest as one of the foolish women speaketh. What? Shall we receive good at the hand of God, and shall we not receive evil? In all this did not Job sin with his lips." Despite his hardships, Job chose to not sin against God with his lips. Understand this—Satan's agenda was to get Job to curse God. Job 1:6-12 tells an all-too-familiar story. It reads, "Now there was a day when the sons of God came to present themselves before the LORD, and Satan came also among them. And the LORD said unto Satan, Whence comest thou? Then Satan answered the LORD, and said, From going to and fro in the earth, and from walking up and down in it. And the LORD said unto Satan, Hast thou considered my servant Job, that there is none like him in the earth, a perfect and an upright man, one that feareth God, and escheweth evil? Then Satan answered the LORD, and said, Doth Job fear God for nought? Hast not thou made an hedge about him, and about his house, and about all that he hath on every side? Thou hast blessed the work of his hands, and his substance is increased in the land. But put forth thine hand now, and touch all that he hath, and he will curse thee to thy face. And the LORD said unto Satan, Behold, all that he hath is in thy power; only upon himself put not forth thine hand. So Satan went forth from the presence of the LORD."

Notice in this scripture that God tells Satan, "All that he has is your power." In other words, he gave Satan a measure of authority over everything and everyone connected to Job. And Satan's goal was to get Job to curse God. This means that his attack was against Job's mind! He wanted to drive Job stir-crazy! The stencil he used was designed to make Job into a blasphemer! So, he attacked him on every side. When Satan decides that he wants you to blaspheme God, he will often attack you in every state in a small window of time. His goal is to convince you that God is unfairly targeting and attacking you or, at minimum, to get you to believe that God doesn't care enough about you to protect you. He wants you to believe that none of your good was good enough for the Most High God. Again, this particular stencil is designed to get you to curse God. People under this mode of attack will often become angry with God, but won't voice their frustrations in the beginning. Slowly, but surely, they will gradually become angrier and angrier at God until they finally respond. The first response often looks like faithlessness or a denunciation of faith. They may say something like, "I don't know if I believe in all that God-stuff anymore." They believe in God, but they are angry with Him! At this stage, vengeance is working through them; they are attempting to put God on punishment because they've humanized Him. They believe or, at minimum, hope that by punishing God, He will realize the error of His ways and stop attacking them or allowing them to be attacked. Of course, He's not attacking them, but this is what the enemy has caused them to believe. Eventually, many of them will commit the sin of blasphemy. This happens when they don't get the help or understanding they need to navigate through the attacks that the enemy has launched against their minds. Notice that Satan did not kill Job's wife. Instead, he used her to accomplish his agenda. Once someone becomes what Satan wants you to be, he will use that person to conform you. This is what he did to Adam; he deformed Eve's thinking and then, used her to pervert her husband's thinking as well. In the midst of her pain and loss, Job's wife found herself at the edge of her sanity, angry with God and ready to embrace death. She'd lost it all, and when she looked up at her husband with bloodshot eyes and tear-stained cheeks, all she could see was him tending to his wounds. In the midst of her own anguish and distress, she opened her mouth and told her husband to curse God. She was one of the many characters who Satan would use in his attempt to accomplish his agenda. The same is true today. Satan has an agenda for every believer and unbeliever. When he looks at you, he's already made a decision as it relates to you. This is why he has surrounded you on every side with narcissists, flying monkeys (apaths) and broken people. Remember, the soul is formable, just as it is transformable, deformable and reformable. Satan puts pressure on the soul with every intent of shaping you into what he's decided that you are to become. So, if he's decided that you are going to be a promiscuous woman who graduates to a destroyer (adulteress), he will hurt you until you no longer trust yourself to be anyone's wife. You see, when a woman becomes a wife, she then begins to teach her man how to be a husband, and not just a husband, but her husband. This isn't the knowledge that he enters the marriage with. She says to him, for example:

- "Take me out at least once a week."
- "Don't yell at me. I prefer to talk about our problems."
- "Why are you walking ahead of me? We're not Muslim. I'm your rib, not your tailbone."
- "Friend? No, I'm your friend and your wife. I don't want her calling you."
- "Touch me here."
- "Don't do that. I hate that."

She even teaches her husband the proper way to satisfy a woman sexually. How so? Sex isn't just rhythmical movements designed to conjure up an orgasm. No. It's intimacy with the mind that expresses itself through the body. Without the intimacy of the mind, sex is just a performance-based event. Believe it or not, married couples regularly enjoy both intimate sex and performance-based sex. So, if a man is preparing to go to work, he may engage in sex with his wife, but this sex is more of a means to an end than anything. This isn't a crime, nor is it a sin; this type of intercourse is all about sexual gratification, and it also helps to create a stronger bond between the couple. But needless to say, it's not as "satisfying" as intimacy, especially for women. Now, let's get an understanding about a mistress, but first, we have to go a little PG-13 again. The vagina of a woman is comprised of horizontal muscles called a pelvic floor. Contrary to popular belief, the muscles in a woman's vagina almost always snap back into place; their elasticity isn't affected by sex. They are normally affected by childbirth and age. But what about those "loose" women that we've heard men joking about? You know, those women who've reportedly lost their abilities to please a man because of their promiscuity? According to science and medicine, they don't exist; at least, not because of promiscuity. Most weakened pelvic floors are the result of childbirth. The concept of a loose woman was a tool designed to shame women who were promiscuous or believed to be come in varying shapes and sizes, therefore, sexual incompatibility can and does exist. Nevertheless, we all know that there are men out there who've left their wives for their mistresses, and their wives were virgins when they'd met them. Their mistresses, on the other hand, had been promiscuous women who'd decided to hang up their promiscuity so that they could promiscuous, however, medical professionals have concluded that the experience of "looseness" was not a female problem; it was a compatibility problem. Women's vaginas be faithful to one man. The problem is, he was somebody's husband. Why then would a man leave his wife to be with a "loose" woman? He didn't. He left his wife for a shape. Let me explain.

Have you ever heard someone say, "He's in pretty bad shape?" When someone says this, that person is normally referring to the body of a man or the mind of a man. Let's deal with the mind. The soul, of course, is comprised of the mind, will and emotions. So, when a man is in "bad shape" mentally, this typically means that he's in a dark place. He's hurting, he's angry or he's both hurt and angry. In other words, his soul has just endured a painful or traumatic event. Trauma is Satan's way of shaping the soul into what he wants it to become. He has a plan for you; he's already decided how he wants you to turn out. But to get you in this shape, he has to deform your thinking. He has to put pressure on your soul. This pressure can be internal (self-inflicted), just as it can be external (brought on by others). Think of it this way—just imagine yourself holding a ball of soft clay. You decide that you want that clay ball to become a square, so to accomplish this, you begin to put pressure on that clay. But what if the clay had muscles? What if it had the ability to bounce back into shape after all the pressure you've put on it? This is a picture of what our soul looks like! It has the ability to withstand some of the greatest traumas, BUT you get to decide the direction that you take after any traumatic event. The pressure to go left when God has told us to go right is called temptation! Refusing to give in to this temptation is called resistance; another word for resistance is long-suffering! James 4:7 reads, "Submit yourselves therefore to God. Resist the devil, and he will flee from you." Any bodybuilder will tell you that resistance helps to build muscle. You need gravity if you want to be strong! You need resistance if you want to be successful! When you give in to this temptation, however, you've entered an event called sin. Sin is the pressure put on a stencil; it is designed to deform the way that you think. If you stay there, your soul will begin to take on the shape of the sin you're in. For example, a married man sleeping with another woman outside of his wife has committed adultery, but if he continues to do this, he then becomes an adulterer. What's the difference? A good man can get caught up in adultery if he makes an unwise decision, for example, one of the tricks, wiles or manipulations of an adulteress is to play the damsel in distress. She may say to a male co-worker of hers, "Janice got it good! She got you and all them muscles at home to help her. As for me, I have to haul a one-hundred pound bed up the stairs in my house by myself, but it's all good. I always manage." In this moment, the man feels pressure being put on his soul. This is called temptation. On one hand, he knows that it is unwise for him to go to this woman's house. On the other hand, he feels a level of guilt and responsibility, so he says, "I can come by this evening and help you move the bed upstairs. Will you be home around six?" The adulteress will then use false humility to get him to relax his standards and drop his guard. The Bible says to guard the heart, but Satan needs this man to lower his guard. She says, "No, that's okay. I got it. I need the exercise anyway. I'm sure I'll be okay." But she's already deployed the use of guilt and flattery, and because he's not guarding his heart, he'll likely insist on coming by. He may have good intentions, but she doesn't.

When he arrives at her home, she will likely answer the door wearing a t-shirt and a pair of jogging pants. Surprised? Don't be! This is a part of her seduction. Again, it's designed to make her appear to have pure motives. It's designed to keep him from stopping at the door; it's designed to get him to advance further into the house or, better yet, advance

further into sin. The man in question lowers his guard and does all the hard work, pulling the bed frame and the mattresses upstairs, and then, he proceeds to assemble the bed. And while he's doing this, the mistress-to-be has escaped to her in-suite bathroom. Three minutes later, he can hear the sound of water running, and it becomes more and more clear that she's now taking a shower. Once she's done, she may exit the bathroom wearing a long t-shirt and some really short pants that can't be seen because of the length of the t-shirt. This is an optical illusion. It is designed to give the effect of her being naked underneath the shirt. The goal is to get the man to fall into lust. He's not an adulterer—yet. But if she plays her cards right, she will be the tool that Satan uses to press him into shape or change his mind. No weapon that is FORMED against thee shall prosper. We all love this scripture, even though we neglect to read it in its entirety. It reads, "'No weapon formed against you shall prosper,
And every tongue which rises against you in judgment you shall condemn. This is the heritage of the servants of the LORD, and their righteousness is from Me,' says the LORD." The mistress-to-be was formed, and then, deformed into a destroyer. Her assignment? To change the shape of that man's thinking so that he'll fall out of agreement with his wife. Remember, two cannot walk together unless they are in agreement. The mistress is a beautiful stencil designed to pervert men and destroy families. The only way he can escape her fangs is to obey God. Matthew 5:28 says, "But I say unto you, that hosoever looketh on a woman to lust after

her hath committed adultery with her already in his heart." While putting the finishing touches on the bed, he looks up and sees her with a toothbrush in her mouth. She's walking around, looking for her remote. She looks high, but can't find it, so she then begins to kneel and look under her dresser. Again, this is all a part of the seduction. The Bible says to flee fornication; the word "flee" means to RUN. This is exactly what Joseph did when Potiphar's wife grabbed him by his cloak. Please note that Joseph wasn't running from Potiphar's wife, he was running from himself. He knew that if he stood there and tried to reason with her, his flesh would have started rising up (pun intended). So, he did what YAHWEH told us to do—he ran. But let's go back to the bedroom of the adulteress. She now smells like a bed of soap and roses. The rap playing on her television set has suddenly slowed down, and now, a little R&B is playing. She moves unusually close to the guy in her attempt to find the remote. And because he didn't run out of the place like he should have, all of a sudden, he finds himself getting aroused. But wait—he's not an adulterer just yet. He finally finishes putting the bed together, and the mistress-to-be is happy. "Wait, let me test it," she says playfully plopping down on the bed face up with her legs dancing in the air. He laughs uncomfortably. "I know what I'm doing, lady. Don't question my work," he jokes. His voice is unusually low, unlike earlier. She knows what this means. It means that her seduction is working. "I'd better be heading out before it gets too late," he says looking at his cell phone. With those words, he slowly begins to put his tools away. His pace signals that he has something on his mind; it signals that he is now acclimating to the atmosphere that has been set. "Wait," she says. "Help me up." She then stretches out her hand for him. He foolishly grabs onto her hand and tries to pull her up, but it doesn't take him long to realize that she's pulling him down towards her. And because he made the foolish decision to go to her house and because he forgot to run like Joseph did, he relaxes his muscles and his standards and falls down on top of her. Once the sin has been completed, he's not an adulterer yet. He simply made a series of foolish mistakes. Satan needs him to agree with adultery; he needs him to see nothing wrong with his behavior or if he does see something wrong with it, Satan needs him to rebel or, better yet, be willing to pay the price (his marriage) associated with it. He needs him to be soul-tied to this woman, not just through sex, but he wants to connect them mentally. He needs the man to be able to relate to the mistress.

Immediately after the sex is finished, the man feels a high level of guilt, shame and fear. "We can't do this again," he says. "I'm married. You know this." The mistress agrees. "I'm sorry," she says. "It was my fault. I pulled you. I made the first move. I got distracted by all them muscles, but it won't happen again." But oh, it will! And when it does, he will start to take the shape of an adulterer. That was his mistress's job. An adulterer cannot and will not remain married; that is, unless he or she truly repents. Satan's desire is to destroy his marriage; this is partly because:

1. He hates marriages since marriage mirrors our relationship with God.
2. He has plans for both people in the union, and being married makes it difficult, if not impossible, for them to become what he's decided that they are to be. "And if one prevails against him, two shall withstand him..."
3. If the couple has children, he has plans for them, but two people who are united in God are too strong for him. "... and a threefold cord is not quickly broken." Always remember these words—Satan thinks in generations!

Satan comes to steal, kill and destroy. A mistress has what's called a destroyer spirit, but remember 1 Peter 5:8. It states, "Be sober, be vigilant; because your adversary the devil, as a roaring lion, walketh about, seeking whom he may devour." This means that he cannot devour everyone. Remember, God placed a hedge of protection around Job, but this hedge of protection was one-sided. Satan could not go past it to get to Job, but had Job stepped outside the will of God, he would have lost what was left of his sanity! Consider the dream I shared with you in Book Four. I was in a room getting my hair and makeup done, but I peered out into the hallway, and that's when I saw three children. They couldn't come in the room where I was, and I somehow knew this, but there was nothing stopping me from leaving that room. I simply chose to stay in the will of God. The same is true for a mistress. She can't break into a man's house and lay between him and his wife. She has to seduce the man to come outside of God's will, and from there, Satan can begin to carry out his deformation process. If Satan has decided that he wants that man to be a murderer, locked up for 25 years to life, he will begin to deform that man's thinking. He has a stencil or a recipe that will ensure that the man in question slowly begins to think and reason as a murderer. It's typically flattery that leads to trauma. So, let's say that Satan uses the poison of obsession to carry out his agenda. The mistress comes into the picture and turns the man's heart away from his wife. Consequently, he begins to mishandle his wife and abuse his marriage until his marriage gives up its ghost and succumbs to an event called divorce. He's now obsessed with his mistress because she's 15 years younger, more energetic and a whole lot wittier than his ex-wife. All the same, she doesn't conform to societal norms, which makes her exciting and mysterious; this arouses and engages the hunter in him. But after his marriage is completely destroyed and his ex-wife is no longer in the picture, the mistress slowly begins to have a change of heart. This is because she is an adulteress! An adulteress needs an adulterer; every other man is just a fill-in. Her job is done, but this is just a beginning. Now damaged in the Eros state, the financial state and mentally, he slowly begins to be ushered into the pits of insanity. His lover isn't answering his calls like she used to, and anytime he stops by her house, she's not at home. His former wife has moved on with her life and remarried, and his children have learned to live without him. Child support is making it difficult for him to give his mistress the life she clearly wants, and now, she's slowly exiting the relationship. One day, he sees her driving a red convertible down the highway, so he follows her. She stops at a gas station to refuel the vehicle, and that's when she sees him. It's clear that he hasn't had a haircut or a shower in at least a week. He confronts her about not answering his calls and questions her about the strange car. "I was busy!" she says childishly. "Oh my gosh, please don't start being clingy! And this car belongs to a friend of mine! She let me borrow it because my car needs new tires! Why must you be so insecure?! Man, stop! Just go home and I'll call you later!" She walks away with him in tow, but it's clear that she's trying to get away from him. Feeling guilty about the way he behaved, he CashApp's her $500 for new tires. A few days later, she blocks his calls because he won't stop calling, texting and being argumentative. Less than a week later, he stops by her house and sees that same red convertible parked in the driveway. He parks on the street in front of her house and calls her, but his number has been blocked. He then downloads a free number app, gets himself a free phone number and calls her. "Hello," she says in a whispered tone. "So, you've blocked me from calling you?" he asks. Recognizing his voice, she suddenly hangs up the phone. Angry, hurt and confused, he exits his vehicle and makes his way towards the back of her house. He's determined to peer in through her bedroom window, and when he does, all of his fears, concerns and suspicions are validated. She's lying on the bed face down, receiving a massage from some muscular, tattoo-covered guy. His heart races as he makes his way back to his car. His anger, hurt, rejection, regret, pride, fear and hatred all come together to create the perfect storm for murder. He opens his glove compartment and pulls out a handgun. As he marches up the driveway, all of the memories of what he's lost suddenly begin to flood his mind. He lost his wife, he lost his house, he lost the respect of his children, he lost a large chunk of his income, plus, his reputation was severely damaged, and for what? He then makes his way through the garage door where he finds the door to the kitchen already unlocked as always. Howbeit, the metal latch on the inside has been placed on the door, but it easily gives way with one powerful kick. And now that the door has flung open, he can hear the sounds of the couple panicking. Less than one minute later, gunshots are heard by the neighbors coming from the house. The former mistress is shot four times and she dies on the scene. Her new lover, on the other hand, is shot twice but survives to tell the story. The killer has finally graduated to becoming what Satan decided that he was to be. He became a murderer, and he was sentenced to 25 years to life. With him out of the way, Satan can now focus on his children. He's already made up his mind about them as well. Now that they are fatherless, it's easier to deform their thinking all the more because there's no credible man in their lives to teach them how to resist the pressure he puts on their minds. As for the guy's ex-wife, her trauma has caused her to distrust men which, consequently causes men who are not trustworthy to be attracted to her. This is a spiritual food chain of sorts. Predators are attracted to prey, just as prey (victims) are attracted to predators. This cycle doesn't end until the victim becomes a victor. Satan decided that he wanted her (the ex-wife) to be an adulteress as well; he wanted to use her to capture the souls (the mind, will and emotions) of men. He's also made this decision in regards to their daughters. But to get them in this shape, he uses their ignorance, a history of trauma and their circle of friends to break and mold them. He also uses culture, premarital sex and the girlfriend tag to deform their thinking. Sex outside of God's will is trauma in disguise!

Let's revisit the discussion of the female anatomy. While such topics may be taboo in the church, we have to learn to get past our discomforts so that we can enter into the vaults of revelation. According to science, a woman's vagina will always return to its original shape regardless of how many men she's slept with and how often she's had intercourse. In other words, the female anatomy is pretty resilient, and it is for this reason that a lot of women engage in promiscuity. (Of course, men do this as well). But here's what you need to know—while your "lady parts" may be resilient, your soul doesn't always bounce back. As a matter of fact, sin wears down your will, thus, causing you to become desensitized to it, but not its effects. Remember, your will is a dimension of your soul. The battleground is in the mind, the weapons used are your emotions and the goal is to hijack your will. Again, sex that happens outside of the confines of God's will is a recipe for trauma. The car dealership may advance you on a vehicle, trusting that you'll eventually pay them their asking price plus interest for the vehicle; a lender may advance you on a loan, trusting that you'll eventually repay the loan with interest, and a bank may advance you on a house, trusting that you'll eventually pay the house and its interest off, but there's no way for you to give another human being an advance on your soul. You see, banks, car dealerships and loan agencies have contracts, lawyers, the backing of the United States government and a methodology to collect all that is owed to them. They have their three-fold cord and then some! They will get your social security number, your banking information, your job's location, your family information and anything that they can gather to ensure the repayment of their advances. But when you engage in sex outside of God's will, you are gambling with your soul, and you can rest assured that the gamble won't return in your favor. You may not be gambling with your salvation, but you are gambling with your mind, will and emotions. Think of it this way—every human being is a stencil. Some people are designed and assigned by God to help you get into shape so that He can use you all the more. This is called impartation. Once you are in the right shape, the windows of Heaven will begin to open and you'll be ready to fit into your next season. But some people have been sent by the enemy to deform your thinking. You may have personally decided that your beau or your girlfriend is "the one" for you, and you may have decided that the two of you are going to get married someday. Consequently, you may be engaging in premarital sex with this person. In your mind, it's okay for him to use and shape you as his wife, or if you're a guy, you may have reasoned that it's okay for her to put her imprint on your soul. But what happens when you realize that the person you're with is not compatible with your future? In other words, that person is a stencil, and as long as he or she is in your life, you will not be able to access your next season! So, you're left with a choice—either you can commit to the season you're in and stay with that person, forsaking your God-given assignment—or you can obey God. People who fit into your region of thought today won't necessarily fit into your tomorrow, and God knows this. This is why He makes us wait! Please don't think that because you're Christian and your insignificant other is Christian that this automatically makes you compatible. It doesn't! I've met plenty of God-fearing, Holy Spirit filled guys who I'm not compatible with. I've met guys in passing, and I didn't even have to exchange phone numbers with them to see that they are incompatible with my future. They were Christian guys with sound minds, but their ideologies and my ideology didn't pair well together. When two people are incompatible, either mentally or sexually, they will traumatize each other or lack the ability to satisfy one another, which in and of itself can be traumatizing. I believe one of the most traumatic events that a person can endure is to be denied access to the next season simply because of someone they are connected to. This is why God told us in Matthew 6:33, "But seek ye first the kingdom of God, and his righteousness; and all these things shall be added unto you." In other words, He's saying, "Let me transform you into who I created you to be; this way, you will qualify for everything that I have in store for you! You won't desire or need void-fillers, nor will you be compatible with people who are incompatible with Me!" But we don't listen, so we have to allow trauma to serve as a disciplinarian in our lives until we have nothing else to lose, but everything to gain from obeying God.

Satan attacks the mind of a person so that he can deform that person's thinking. I like to think of all of the sins as stencils or cookie cutters. If he decides that he wants you to be a drug dealer, he has a stencil or a recipe for that. He knows how much pressure and pain it will take to get you into that shape. He wanted Job to curse God, but he failed at getting him to do so because Job didn't bend to the pressure; instead, he resisted. In other words, he was like a dent that kept popping back out. And again, he'd deformed a promiscuous woman into a destroyer (adulteress) by causing her to go through hurt, rejection, abandonment, betrayal and any other soul stencil that he can find. Once he got her into the shape he wanted her in, he then caused her to harden her heart. This makes her stubborn, prideful, hardhearted and unwilling to hear the truth. This also solidifies her in the purpose he's given her. Her job is to then reproduce herself. The male version of an adulteress is an adulterer. So, all of a sudden, she's no longer interested in single men; instead, she finds herself attracted to married men. But remember, the wife has educated her husband regarding what it takes to truly take care of a woman—body, mind and soul. These traits aren't just attractive to his wife, but they are attractive to women as a whole, especially adulteresses. He is a ready-made meal! All the same, the mistress's soul is weak; the enemy has advanced into many of her states and weakened her defense. Because of this, she's likely weak in the areas of finance, family, romance, faith and every other state. She doesn't have the knowledge or the patience to be anybody's wife, especially if she has to teach a man how to truly love her. Another analogy to consider is this—imagine that she can't cook, so she's always in the freezer section of her local supermarket, looking for meals that other folks have already prepared. So, she goes after married men, thinking that she can steal their wives' lives and identities, after all, this is what the mistress is after. She looks at the wife and envies her life, all but the fact that she's being cheated on. Howbeit, in her ignorance, she blames the wife for the fact that her husband is in the shape he's in. What she doesn't realize is that Satan is using her to change his mind; that is, to change the shape of his soul, therefore, making him incompatible with his wife. She is a stencil used by the enemy to get the man into a specific state of mind; this way, the enemy can fulfill his agenda with that man. In other words, even if she gets the man, she will never have with him what he had with this wife, and Satan knows this, after all, everything that is built has to be maintained. For example, a wife will often remind her husband, for example:

- "I told you to take me out at least once a week."
- "We talk about our problems, remember? We don't yell."
- "I'm your rib, not your tailbone. Walk with me, not ahead of me, please."

- "I don't want her calling you. I don't trust her."
- "Don't touch me like that. Touch me like this."
- "Don't do that. I hate that."

The mistress, on the other hand, assumes that the man is naturally good with women, but this isn't necessarily true. His soul or way of thinking will pop back into its original form, and she will have to take on the difficult task of communicating what she wants with him. For most mistresses, this is a nightmare; it's too much work. They often deal with entitlement, so they want everything prepared and handed to them, including men. This mode of thinking ensures the destruction of their relationship. So, when the man begins to return to the shape he was in before his wife started coaching him; in other words, he begins to sober up, most adulteresses will go on the hunt looking for another ready-made meal.

Proverbs 4:7-27
Say unto wisdom, Thou art my sister; and call understanding thy kinswoman: That they may keep thee from the strange woman, from the stranger which flattereth with her words. For at the window of my house I looked through my casement, and beheld among the simple ones, I discerned among the youths, a young man void of understanding, passing through the street near her corner; and he went the way to her house, in the twilight, in the evening, in the black and dark night: And, behold, there met him a woman with the attire of an harlot, and subtil of heart.

(She is loud and stubborn; her feet abide not in her house: Now is she without, now in the streets, and lieth in wait at every corner.) So she caught him, and kissed him, and with an impudent face said unto him, I have peace offerings with me; this day have I paid my vows. Therefore came I forth to meet thee, diligently to seek thy face, and I have found thee. I have decked my bed with coverings of tapestry, with carved works, with fine linen of Egypt. I have perfumed my bed with myrrh, aloes, and cinnamon. Come, let us take our fill of love until the morning: let us solace ourselves with loves. For the goodman is not at home, he is gone a long journey: He hath taken a bag of money with him, and will come home at the day appointed. With her much fair speech she caused him to yield, with the flattering of her lips she forced him. He goeth after her straightway, as an ox goeth to the slaughter, or as a fool to the correction of the stocks; till a dart strike through his liver; as a bird hasteth to the snare, and knoweth not that it is for his life. Hearken unto me now therefore, O ye children, and attend to the words of my mouth. Let not thine heart decline to her ways, go not astray in her paths. For she hath cast down many wounded: yea, many strong men have been slain by her. Her house is the way to hell, going down to the chambers of death.

Consider your own trauma. Please note that everything the enemy did to you had purpose attached to it. Whether you were raped, molested, rejected, abandoned, abused or whatever methodology the enemy used to deform your thinking, it is important for you to know that the attack wasn't random. He was attacking your mind, and this is because he has a plan for you that's older than you are. Whatever he has determined in regards to you, he has a series of stencils that he will use and has used to get you into the shape he wants you to be in. Sometimes, the stencil comes in the form of an adulterer or an adulteress; sometimes, it comes in the shape of a friend. And in many cases, it comes in the form of a toxic parent. All the same, his favorite weapon is called rejection, whether that rejection comes from strangers or the people we love and trust. But there's a simple way to deal with this—if someone holds their love, attention, affirmation and acceptance over your head, it's not worth having. Yes, including your parents! Change your mind and move on! Think of it this way. Let's say that you went to college and received a Master's Degree in Psychology. And now, you're working on your Ph.D. You apply to work at a psychiatric hospital, and of course, you are qualified for many of the positions that are open, but the hiring manager takes one look at you and says, "The only position we have open is in maintenance. And we're paying $11,000 a year. Do you want the job or not?" You can be making, at minimum, $70,000 a year, but the woman sitting across from you is trying to devalue your education. Would you take the job? No, you wouldn't! You'd go and look elsewhere. You have to apply that same line of reasoning when it comes to relationships, whether they are platonic, romantic or familial. If you're being yourself and someone rejects the authentic you, that person has no space in his or her life for you, and that person isn't willing to create space for you. In other words, that person is NOT called to your life or vice versa! Chances are, that person is what I call a molder. A molder is an individual who has mastered a region of thought; they are skilled at picking and manipulating people. These people are full of voids and pride. Molders only accept people who are willing to be conformed so they can fit into the roles they have available. They don't like authenticity; they are insecure around everyone who dares to be their authentic selves. Because confident people make them uncomfortable, they strategically surround themselves with people whose self-esteem have been defeated. These are the cliques that you'll find pooling around each other in every given region of thought. And again, you may have wanted to be accepted; you may have hoped to fit in, but it was not the will of God for you to conform because conformation is a perversion of the mind and an enemy of purpose.

And lastly, ask yourself these questions:
- What did I take from the trauma?
- Am I still connected to toxic people?
- What is my strategy for dealing with mentally unstable people?

Understand that you need a plan of action, after all, Satan is strategic, but most church folks are emotional. This is why so many believers fail to manifest the blessings and favor of God in their lives. Promotion in the Kingdom requires us all to have bloody altars. We have to be willing to move when

God tells us to move, to stay when God tells us to be still and to let go of everything and everyone that God tells us to release. Most believers try to sing, dance and shout their way around this. The Word of God works, but we all have to remember that, while we can master regions of thought, we can never master God. In other words, we cannot manipulate Him or trick Him into giving us the desires of our hearts. This is why He says in Isaiah 55:9, "For as the heavens are higher than the earth, so are my ways higher than your ways, and my thoughts than your thoughts." Everything He has for you and me is within the confines of His will and His timing. In other words, you may have mastered a season, and consequently, you may have become a mastermind in that region of thought, but you don't have the words, the knowledge or the power to manipulate the Most High God. This means you have to study His Word, have faith and try Him at His Word. Every other tool is ineffective. All the same, He has plans for you, of course, but it is never wise to chase the hand of God without first getting His heart. A lot of believers are traumatized today because they chased riches, relationships, platforms and success, not realizing that NONE of these things can satisfy a broken soul.

1 Timothy 6:9: But those who desire to be rich fall into temptation and a snare, and into many foolish and harmful lusts which drown men in destruction and perdition.

SEASONAL ASYLUMS

One of the things that's on my bucket list is to go into an asylum one day or several asylums with a team of God-fearing, Holy Spirit filled believers who are not afraid of demons. I want to watch God clean out that entire asylum (or most of it), and of course, I don't want to just do this one time. I would love to shut down every mental institution that serves as a prison, a cave, a safe-house or a grave to many of God's prophets, apostles and every other person called to serve Him in a ministerial capacity. You see, many of the people in these institutions are gifted, but broken. Most of them have traumatic backgrounds that stretch all the way into their childhoods. As I mentioned in Book Four, when I was ten years old, I kept having a series of dreams. In these dreams, there was a metal fence that stretched all the way to Heaven; you could not see where it started or ended, either vertically or horizontally. I was on one side of the fence, but on the other side stood a fair-skinned young boy who was around my age. He had a lot of freckles on his face and his hair was cut low. In every one of these dreams, he would just stare at me, gripping the gate and following me whenever I walked to the left or the right. He was a demon; I now know this now, but when I was a child, I wanted to remove that fence because he looked like he cared about me. The fence was symbolic of three things:

1. **God's protection.** Even though he clearly had some

measure of access to me, he wasn't allowed to touch my life. The fence was a hedge of protection; it was a standard that stopped the devil from doing the amount of damage he wanted to do. What I didn't mention in the previous edition was that these dreams started not long after I had been violently raped by a neighbor. The enemy clearly had a plan for my life, and even though he had already launched his attack against me, he did not have the amount of access he needed to kill me, steal my identity, rob me of my purpose or silence my voice.

2. **Generational bondage.** This is the horizontal direction of the fence. I couldn't see where the fence started or stopped. This symbolized generations upon generations of bondage that I would be fighting against in my own bloodline! Being born into the poorest state (Mississippi) to poor parents was the least of my issues. The demons that were in my family had never been addressed, and there were MANY of them. But God showed me this because He was going to use me to be a curse-breaker in my family.

3. **Godly authority.** The fence reached up to Heaven—or could it be that the fence reached down to Earth? The devil-boy being on the other side of the fence represented him being bound. You can't legally bind someone without the authority to do so. This was a clear picture of my future. God would eventually use me to capture and bind unclean spirits, not just in myself, but in His people.

Notice that I said he "looked" like he cared about me. At that time, I was a child so I wasn't mature enough to understand that what was staring at me from the other side of that fence was not holy and it wanted to destroy me. But because I was young and immature, if I could have removed that fence, I would have. And if I had removed that fence, I'd either be dead or crazy today; either way, the fence was set in place to protect me. It was a standard. Isaiah 59:19 says, "So shall they fear the name of the Lord from the west, and his glory from the rising of the sun. When the enemy shall come in like a flood, the Spirit of the Lord shall lift up a standard against him." Merriam Webster's online dictionary defines the word "standard" as "a conspicuous object (such as a banner) formerly carried at the top of a pole and used to mark a rallying point, especially in battle or to serve as an emblem." Our standard as believers is the blood-soaked banner that God availed to us through His Son, Jesus Christ. And while I wasn't yet saved, the standard placed on me had been done through the power of intercession. You see, my great-grandmother had been a powerful prayer warrior who loved God with all of her heart. She used to babysit me when my parents went to work; she did this all the way up until her death. I was six-years old when she passed away, but I still have memories of her. My dad's mother died when she was 24, so my great-grandparents raised him and his siblings, and according to my dad, they were relatively wealthy. My great-grandparents owned two businesses; one was a thrift shop and I think the other was a shoe restoration shop. I remember going to the thrift shop with my great-grandmother on several occasions. I would play in the store while she worked. My favorite game was to hide in the middle of the racks between the clothes until she called me out. I still remember the smell of that shop and the smell of shoe polish. I also remember her taking me to church with her on several occasions. I was somewhat uncomfortable at her church because the people danced violently around the church. They ran laps, screamed, passed out and danced with all of their might. This scared and intrigued me at the same time. But one day, while praying for another child (as an adult), I heard God say, "She prayed for you." All of a sudden, I had a vision of me being in my great-grandmother's church, and in that vision, I had oil on my forehead. Again, she died when I was six-years old, and til this day, I am still reaping the benefits of her prayers. That fence that I saw in my dream when I was ten-years old was likely the product of her intercession. Of course, it was established by God, but she birthed it in the earth through intercession when she was alive.

The purpose of a purity cloth was for a husband and a wife to consummate their marriage on, but the function of the cloth was to protect, not just the bride from the accusation of her husband, but it also protected the name of her father. If a husband accused his wife (which was relatively commonplace in that day) of not being a virgin when he'd met her, he was also in that same breath accusing her father of being an immoral man. This would do irreparable damage to his name and his reputation, so if a husband tried to get out of his marriage by lying on his wife, her father would show up to the meeting holding the blood-stained banner that was her purity cloth. By doing so, he would clear his daughter's name and restore the people's trust in him. The husband would then have to pay one hundred shekels to the father of the bride. Deuteronomy 22:18-19 (ESV) details his punishment. It reads, "Then the elders of that city shall take the man and whip him, and they shall fine him a hundred shekels of silver and give them to the father of the young woman, because he has brought a bad name upon a virgin of Israel. And she shall be his wife. He may not divorce her all his days." This is reminiscent of Proverbs 6:30-31 (ESV), which reads, "People do not despise a thief if he steals to satisfy his appetite when he is hungry, but if he is caught, he will pay sevenfold; he will give all the goods of his house." The same is true for us; whenever we find the thief (Satan) operating in our lives and we hold up the blood-stained banner, Satan not only has to release what he was trying to steal, he has to restore everything he's stolen from us and our families! Everything attached to your father's name that has been released by God to you has to suddenly be released by the enemy. Consider the story of Daniel. He'd been praying to God because of a word he'd received. He decided to push that prayer through by fasting. Twenty-one days later, he had an encounter with an angel of God. Daniel 10:10-14 (ESV) tells the story. It reads, "And behold, a hand touched me and set me trembling on my hands and knees. And he said to me, 'O Daniel, man greatly loved, understand the words that I speak to you, and stand upright, for now I have been sent to you.' And when he had spoken his word to me, I stood up trembling. Then he said to me, 'Fear not, Daniel, for from the first day that you set your heart to understand and humbled yourself before your God, your words have been heard, and I have come because of your words. The prince of the kingdom of Persia withstood me twenty-one days, but Michael, one of the chief princes, came to help me, for I was left there with the kings of Persia, and came to make you understand what is to happen to your people in the latter days. For the vision is for days to come.'" The point I want you to see is that the enemy does hold up blessings; the Bible calls him a thief because that's what he his, howbeit, when we call on the name of Jesus, Satan has to loose whatever he's been holding, BUT get this—you may not be mature enough to receive what he's stolen from your family. If and when this happens, Satan still has to release it, but it will wait for you in its assigned season. Consider what the angel said to Daniel. "The vision is for days to come." In other words, not yet!

God lifts a standard or measure of rule against the enemy; we've established this, and even though the standard keeps the enemy in check, the believer also has to honor that boundary. When the enemy can't get to you, he will try to coerce you into coming to him. Remember the story of Job—Satan's objective was to get Job to curse God, but Job didn't fall into this trap. God told Satan that everything Job had was in his hands, but Satan was not allowed to touch his life. In other words, the devil couldn't kill him. This was the standard, but had Job cursed God, he would have died. And this is what Satan wanted; this is why he frustrated the wife until she said to Job, "Curse God and die." The point is, God can and does place boundaries around us, and the enemy stands on the other side of that fence, trying to get our attention so that we will come outside of God's will. He will use every seducing technique that he can think of, including disguising himself as an angel of light or disguising himself as the man or woman of our dreams, a best friend, an opportunity or whatever it is that we refuse to live without. Sadly enough, many believers have fallen into this trap, and consequently, some have lost their lives, while others have lost the soundness of their minds. Our asylums are filled with prophets and prophetic people who touched something that God told them not to touch, went somewhere that God told them not to go or did something that God told them not to do. Or their parents disobeyed God, and consequently, they were born into the ditches their parents dug for them. And today, there are believers and unbelievers out there who are literally married to folks that Satan sent to bind and blind them. We stood at their weddings watching them put a ring on each other's fingers, but we couldn't see the yoke-turned-nooses that were being placed around their necks. Who do you think Delilah was? She was a weapon formed against the purpose, the assignment and the life of Samson. Who do you think Jezebel was? She was a weapon formed against Ahab's legacy and the kingdom of Israel. Think about the many men in the Old Testament who married women, got bored with them and decided to lie their way out of their covenants. They went and accused their wives before the elders, knowing what the consequence would be should their wives be found guilty. Of course, the accusation was that the women had already engaged in sexual intercourse before they'd married them, thus, making her ineligible to be married to another man. If the wives or their fathers had not put the purity clothes away in a safe place, and if the woman was found guilty of this crime, she'd be taken to her father's house and stoned to death right in front of his door! Her father would forever be seen as an immoral man, and no one would agree to do business with him or his children. In other words, being rejected by society was the equivalent of what we call a generational curse today! This is the price that the wife and her family would have had to pay if the lie was able to stand! This is all because the guy got bored and decided that he didn't want to be married anymore! Narcissism isn't something that's new; that demon has been around since Satan and his crew got kicked out of Heaven!

Again, there are believers in mental institutions till this day because they dishonored the boundaries that had been put in place to protect them. One such boundary we all have, of course, is to not practice dark arts; another word for dark arts is witchcraft. Witchcraft is oftentimes the product of impatience, unforgiveness, bitterness, jealousy and pride. When these five come together, they produce the storms that we identify as depression, frustration, anxiety, anger, fear, and the list goes on. This is why the Bible tells us to be anxious for nothing. One of Satan's most effective traps is unforgiveness, but just like every other drug, it has an active ingredient. The active ingredient is blame; this is caused by a lack of accountability; another word for this is deflection. Merriam Webster defines the word "deflect" as "to turn (something) aside, especially from a straight course or fixed direction." Remember, we are all advancing towards a purpose; we are going or growing from one region of thought to the next. This is a straight course and oftentimes, we deviate from this path in an event called sin. When this happens, in order to get back on course, we have to repent. The word "repent" means to turn around or change directions. It means to get back on the right path, which is the straight and narrow path. Saying that you're sorry but refusing to take responsibility for your wrongs is not true repentance; it's called deflecting. Taking accountability, on the other hand, is called reflecting. Both have to deal with the direction of your heart. If your heart is headed in the wrong direction, you are not advancing forward, but are instead returning to the vomit that God delivered you from. The direction of your heart will determine where you end up. If you are heading in the wrong direction, you are heading towards whatever it is that God has delivered you from personally and generationally. This is why we see so many of us African Americans returning to witchcraft; this is a generational issue that many of our forefathers struggled with because they lacked knowledge. Nowadays, when we are trying to rediscover our roots, we don't go back far enough. Instead, we trace our ancestry back to the ancestors who practiced ancestral worship and other dark arts; consequently, we see an uprise in people embracing things like the use of sage to combat evil spirits, necromancy, astrology and the like. This has everything to with the direction that we are heading in! God didn't tell us to go backwards, He told us to repent. In other words, He told us to come forward! The word "come" is an invitation! He has invited us into places that we are not qualified for, but just like any other invitation, we have to accept it. He wants us to advance in the Kingdom so that we can advance the Kingdom, but the enemy uses every method and tool he has to advance in us. But remember, he can't do this unless he gets you outside of God's will, and not just through works; again, your works or decisions are fruits. Every fruit has a root, and every root was produced by a seed! Every farmer knows that if you pick all the apples from an apple tree, they will eventually grow back! The point is, the way to keep a sound mind or, as we say in today's terminology, a sane mind, we have to move with God through an event called agreement. There's no neutrality in spirituality; either you are with God or against Him. There is no middle ground!

Again, one of my desires is to walk into a series of mental institutions or asylums and just start praying for people, and I'm sure many leaders have had this very same desire. Howbeit, the reason this hasn't been done yet is because, as we all come to mature in Christ, we come to understand that deliverance is much more than just screaming at demons. It has everything to do with the direction of a person's heart, whether that person is walking with God or against Him.

Sadly enough, many of the people that are institutionalized decided to walk against Him. Then again, many of them are there because they crossed a boundary while walking with Him that He told them not to cross, and they did this repeatedly. In other words, they were pride-filled and rebellious. And it goes without saying that not every mentally unstable person is institutionalized. Some of the craziest people alive are living amongst us, and many of them hold positions of power. For example, have you ever had that very condescending, competitive, drama-loving boss who hated you for no other reason than the fact that you took a breath without his or her permission? You know that boss who didn't like anyone except the employees who were loud, angry and violent? This is because your boss was just like the people that he or she favored! This was your boss's institution! An institution is nothing but a gathering of minds, whether it be a mental institution or a familial institution, all the way up to a religious institution. In every institution, there are levels; for example, in a mental institution, they have floors that house the most mentally deranged people, just as they have floors and staff for people who aren't necessarily considered a threat to themselves or society. In a familial institution, you'll see cliques or people who pool around each other every time the family gathers. The same is true in a religious institution. After church has ended, you'll see pools of people gathering together. You'll see closed circles; these are the people who have decided that they don't want any new members in their cliques, oftentimes because of fear, distrust, comparison or personal preferences. You'll see open circles; these are the people who invite you over with their eyes, their body language or sometimes with a gesture. These are your more open-minded people. What you are seeing is the gathering of sound and unsound minds. These are the levels of that institution. Every clique represents a level or a floor, but get this—the most powerful cliques aren't necessarily the soundest! Think about a prison institution. The most powerful prisoners are oftentimes the craziest ones there. The same is sometimes true in spirituality. The more spiritual you are, the closer you are edging towards insanity, at least, by the world's standards. This is why so many believers try to have what they call "balanced learning." They try to offset what they've experienced and learned spiritually by engaging in what some would call carnality. Then again, there are the ones who venture so far off into spirituality that they become weird, unrelatable AND sometimes even potent. Consider what the word "potent" means when, for example, you're dealing with alcohol. It means that there is no additive to take away its power or effect. It means to be undiluted. Consequently, the more potent you are as a leader, the less friends you'll have; this is because you're on a different floor or level than most people. Consequently, people will see you as strange, crazy, problematic or unrelatable. Please note that most people who can't relate to you don't want to relate to you; this is why becoming more spiritual is your choice. Many of us are called, but every call requires an answer. Can you imagine how "weird" Moses must've appeared to the people, especially after he'd spent forty days and forty nights in the presence God? Can you imagine how "weird" David must've looked when he danced right out of his clothes? So yes, you can be spiritual and not crazy, BUT you need a guide. For example, I want to go to Africa in 2021 or 2022, but it would be silly for me to go there without a guide. Wherever I go, I have to make sure that I have someone who's familiar with that place to lead me around; this way, I won't put myself in harm's way. The same is true for spirituality. You need a pastor! And if your pastor is not versed in the arena of spirituality that you're interested in like deliverance, healing or the prophetic, you should get yourself a mentor, but make sure that you are fully accountable to your pastor. So, if I decided that I wanted to be mentored by a leader who, for example, who is strong in the areas that I want to be strong in, I wouldn't just go and ask that person to mentor me. No, I'd consult with my pastors, letting them know my desires and my intentions. Why? Isn't this idolatry? No, it's called accountability! Hebrews 13:17 reads, "Obey them that have the rule over you, and submit yourselves: for they watch for your souls, as they that must give account, that they may do it with joy, and not with grief: for that is unprofitable for you." The ESV version translates it this way, "Obey your leaders and submit to them, for they are keeping watch over your souls, as those who will have to give an account. Let them do this with joy and not with groaning, for that would be of no advantage to you." Some of the folks who are "certified" as insane today are people who were lone-runners; they didn't think they needed a pastor or they needed their pastors' attention. So, they went to every spiritual event that arose in their cities and ended up getting bound! They wouldn't listen to direction, and anyone who told them to be accountable to their pastors was ridiculed by them. "He put his pants on one leg at a time just like me!" they shouted. And now, they are being placed in straitjackets. I can't tell you how many coaching sessions I've had with people like this! They didn't think they needed permission or any level of accountability, and now, they are convinced that the United States government has FBI and CIA agents stalking and following them! In other words, they have lost the soundness of their minds! And when people get like this, it is nearly impossible to convince them otherwise, especially when they back their beliefs with scriptures taken out of context, false prophecies, misunderstood prophecies or when they claim to have had some sort of spiritual encounter. All the same, I have worked with thousands of ministries, so it goes without saying that I've met my fair share of folks who've stepped out on the water without Jesus. In other words, they tried to go ahead of God and ended up over their heads. Can they be recovered? Yes, but they'll have to repent. Remember, the word "repent" means to turn around; it means to return to your agreement with God.

And lastly, a season can become an asylum if you don't get out of it when God calls you out. Anytime you master a season, you become a mastermind of that particular region of thought, a crafty person or an expert of that season. Again, another word for this is manipulator. The most manipulative people I've met are the ones who have mastered an institution, whether that institution is the institution of family, government, etc. This is because anytime you enter a season, it's only natural for you to be attracted to the folks at the top of that season; these are the people who know their way around a region of thought and they know the who's who of that region. They have influence and power within that season, and they are oftentimes drunk on this power. This is why they won't humble themselves and grow. They don't want to enter new seasons where they are the babes, the unlearned or the newbies needing direction. They love being at the height of their last seasons; they love being at the top of the bottom. And these are oftentimes the people who will give you the most opposition should you begin to grow outside of their influence, and I'm not talking about your spiritual leaders, after all, you should be submitted to them. You should be taking direction from them. I'm talking about people who have absolutely nothing to do with your faith-walk or your growth, but somehow feel entitled to the number one position in everything. They are very strategic regarding who they hang around; every move they make is a power move. They treat successful men and women like kings and queens, but they are often very dismissive of the people who don't have any influence or power (at least in their minds) or the people they feel shouldn't have any influence or power. If they're upset with you, you'll notice that a lot of people within that arena aren't speaking to you; if they're celebrating you, you'll notice that a lot of people within that arena are trying to connect with you. They use their power and influence for evil; they use their power to get their way. And this is why they are oftentimes your biggest opposers whenever you start growing through a season that they've mastered. You will find this group in every region of thought that you grow through! These are the people who Apostle Paul was speaking of in 1 Corinthians 1:27-29 when he said, "But God chose what is foolish in the world to shame the wise; God chose what is weak in the world to shame the strong; God chose what is low and despised in the world, even things that are not, to bring to nothing things that are, so that no human being might boast in the presence of God." They are the wise, the strong and the sought out in any given region of thought. In other words, their wisdom has become their strongholds and their last season has become their asylums. Think about the "get off my grass" neighbors that many of us have had. For example, that pride-filled woman living in a safe section of a bad neighborhood who drives a Cadillac and treats everyone around her like they're beneath her. She's normally outside everyday or every few days watering her flowers, washing her car or yelling at the neighborhood kids. She refuses to greet her neighbors or respond to them whenever they greet her. And whenever one of the children in her neighborhood does anything she disapproves of, she will berate the child, scold the mother or call the cops. Believe it or not, she's mentally ill. She may not be certifiably crazy (that is by the world's standards), but she is mentally unstable, which is why she's so prideful and emotional. Most women like this have been abandoned by their children because of their narcissism. They're stuck in the good section of a bad neighborhood, and fifteen to twenty years later, you'll look back and still see that same Cadillac parked in her driveway should you drive through the neighborhood. Eventually, she won't be able to keep up with mowing the grass as she ages, and her lack of trust for people will be the reason that her lawn is overgrown. It's a sad story and a common one as well, and while many of us have gotten upset with people like this, the truth of the matter is, they need love and they need healing. This is what it looks like to get stuck in a region of thought or a neighborhood of thinking.

As you grow through each season, you have to resist the temptation to become comfortable, prideful, entitled and hardhearted. When you reach the height of any given season, it's because you have gotten all the knowledge that you need to graduate from that season. There's a temptation, a snare or a trap at the edge of every season; it's called pride! This is why 1 Corinthians 8:1 (NIV) says, "But knowledge puffs up while love builds up." At the peak of every season is when you'll face your greatest temptation. In that moment, your knowledge will qualify you for power and influence. All of a sudden, people are looking up to you and taking direction from you. It is very easy to get drunk off this power; it is very easy to use this power and influence to accomplish your own agenda. It is very easy to use this power to oppress and oppose people, especially the people who've oppressed and opposed you. It is very easy for your season to become your asylum. The moment pride begins to take ownership of you, you have to resist and overcome it by loving people. This is what qualifies you for your next season. James 4:6 warns us this way, "God resisteth the proud, but giveth grace unto the humble." God resists the proud, but remember that it is knowledge that puffs up! God said that His people perish for lack of knowledge! So, we are supposed to get knowledge, but with all of this getting, He said that we must also get understanding. Additionally, wisdom is the principal or most important thing. Knowledge breeds familiarity, and while we need it, we also have to balance it with understanding and manifest it with wisdom. In other words, we can be masterminds of the seasons that we're in and have God to resist us or we can be students of our next seasons and have God to approve us. We can either be at the top of the bottom or the bottom of the top! People who get stuck in a season because of pride are not sober-minded; they become stiff-necked, entitled and arrogant. Consequently, they start dealing with the strongmen of depression, anxiety, fear and a whole host of spirits. They often feel constricted because they have truly outgrown their seasons, and yet, they refuse to graduate from them because they like being at the top of their class. Learn from them and keep growing! Keep humbling yourself, studying the Word, honoring your leaders and forgiving your enemies! And when you get to the height of any given season, please know that you are now a leader within that realm. Don't utilize that opportunity to get folks to follow you. Instead, lead them by exiting that season. This is why God hates pride. It forms a hard layer around a person's heart, and that person then becomes a wall used by the enemy to keep others from progressing. When people become prideful, God begins to resist them, and because of this, they start losing their peace or the soundness of their minds. These are the folks that we see sitting at the front of most churches wearing five layers of eyeliner, over-sized hats and pointed bras. They are often the meanest and most condescending folks you'll ever come across; this is because they are stuck. Another word for "stuck" is "constipated." Spiritually constipated people are folks who've been eating the revelation from their last season when God wanted to give them fresh revelation. Keep moving, keep loving, keep growing, and more than anything, stay humble!

2 Timothy 3:1-7 (ESV): But understand this, that in the last days there will come times of difficulty. For people will be lovers of self, lovers of money, proud, arrogant, abusive, disobedient to their parents, ungrateful, unholy, heartless, unappeasable, slanderous, without self-control, brutal, not loving good, treacherous, reckless, swollen with conceit, lovers of pleasure rather than lovers of God, having the appearance of godliness, but denying its power. Avoid such people.

1 Peter 5:8-9 (ESV): Be sober-minded; be watchful. Your adversary the devil prowls around like a roaring lion, seeking someone to devour. Resist him, firm in your faith, knowing that the same kinds of suffering are being experienced by your brotherhood throughout the world.

EMBRACING YOUR EXODUS

Exodus 14:15-18

And the LORD said unto Moses, Wherefore criest thou unto me? speak unto the children of Israel, that they go forward: But lift thou up thy rod, and stretch out thine hand over the sea, and divide it: and the children of Israel shall go on dry ground through the midst of the sea. And I, behold, I will harden the hearts of the Egyptians, and they shall follow them: and I will get me honour upon Pharaoh, and upon all his host, upon his chariots, and upon his horsemen. And the Egyptians shall know that I am the LORD, when I have gotten me honour upon Pharaoh, upon his chariots, and upon his horsemen.

Exodus 14:21-25

And Moses stretched out his hand over the sea; and the LORD caused the sea to go back by a strong east wind all that night, and made the sea dry land, and the waters were divided. And the children of Israel went into the midst of the sea upon the dry ground: and the waters were a wall unto them on their right hand, and on their left. And the Egyptians pursued, and went in after them to the midst of the sea, even all Pharaoh's horses, his chariots, and his

Exodus 14:21-25

horsemen. And it came to pass, that in the morning watch the LORD looked unto the host of the Egyptians through the pillar of fire and of the cloud, and troubled the host of the Egyptians, And took off their chariot wheels, that they drave them heavily: so that the Egyptians said, Let us flee from the face of Israel; for the LORD fighteth for them against the Egyptians.

Can you imagine this moment? Can you imagine watching a sea split open right in front of your eyes, all the while, running from an army of men who's hellbent on bringing you back into captivity? The Israelites were standing at the edge of one season, about to enter the hallway of the next season. There was no turning back now! And I'm sure there were many of them who truly wanted to throw their hands in the air and let the Egyptians take them back to the captivity that they'd learned to revere as normal. Nevertheless, Moses stood in front of the sea, being led by God, and the people followed him as he followed the Lord. Were they afraid? Of course! But they had to walk across that Red Sea while their legs trembled, their hearts raced and their stomachs twisted into knots. This was anxiety on its highest setting, and yet, by the mercies of God, they walked out of Egypt and into the space that separated them from their next season. But just like many of us today, they spent a lot of time in the hallway between two seasons because they were double-minded and they wouldn't stop looking back.

If we had an aerial view of the Israelites coming out of the Red Sea and entering into the outer courts of their next season, this picture would look a lot like a woman giving birth. This is because God was birthing them out of an old season and into a new one, but remember, a season is a mindset. He'd already proven Himself to be God and to be more powerful than their oppressor, Pharaoh, but it was up to them to accept Him and give Him His proper place in their hearts. Nevertheless, they looked, smelled and acted so much like their last seasons that they stayed in the birth canal for forty years. Many of them perished in the hallway between their next season and their last season because they complained about being delivered. How many women and men do you know who's doing this to this very day? They are complaining about being single and delivered from the folks who Satan sent to oppress them! So, they stay in the hallway far longer than God wanted to keep them there because they still smell like the folks they sinned with! They won't forgive their Pharaohs and move on. Consequently, they spent forty years going in circles. A circle is a cycle; it looks like a woman dating the same devil in a different man time and time again until she learns to respect the season that she's in. The purpose of the hallway or the wilderness is to remove the scent and the culture of your last season; it is not there to punish you. It's put in place to clean you up before you show up in your next season.

Or course, Harriet Tubman is often referred to as the Black Moses. She helped to free more than three hundred slaves after embarking on 19 missions between the North and the South. The Underground Railroad was the Red Sea that God opened for her to accomplish this mission. And like Moses, Harriet dealt with her fair share of complainers; these were people who didn't want to move forward, but instead, chose to go back. The Israelites could not go back to Egypt because the Red Sea had closed and God wasn't going to reopen it for them. All the same, it was reported that Harriet Tubman carried a pistol with her; this was not only for her protection and the protection of the slaves she was rescuing, but she also used it to threaten weak-minded slaves who wanted to go back to their masters. Knowing that allowing them to do so would compromise the location of the Underground Railroad, Mrs. Tubman is said to have pulled that gun a few times, letting her crew know that they would either advance forward or be killed. In other words, there was no going back! Consider this—in order for Harriet to free anyone, she first had to free herself, but her freedom would come at a price. One of the sacrifices that she had to make was the loss of her marriage. Her husband refused to come out of bondage, but this didn't stop her from getting her freedom. She tried to convince him on a few occasions to follow her, but he refused. He remained the property of his master and would eventually remarry another bound woman. There's a lesson here and that is, bound people are attracted to bound people. This is why you shouldn't get married or even court while you're still in bondage. Get free first; this way, you won't marry someone who's bound, only to discover that they don't want to be free! The price of freedom can sometimes be very high, and very few people are willing to pay it. Can you imagine what would have happened had Harriet chosen her husband over her mission and assignment? More than three hundred people would have remained in bondage, and God would have had to raise up another deliverer. Like Moses, she said yes to the call on her life, despite what it would cost her. And today, she is the most famous African American in United States history.

The first slaves were brought to the United States in 1619. Between 1774 and 1804, slavery had been abolished in all of the Northern states, but it was still active in the Southern states. That is, until Abraham Lincoln took the office as President of the United States. He was anti-slavery and his views were strongly opposed by the South. Within seven months of his presidency, seven Southern states had seceded to create the Confederates States of America. Eventually, that number grew to eleven. It is no surprise that these states were Alabama, Arkansas, Florida, Georgia, Louisiana, Mississippi, North Carolina, South Carolina, Tennessee, Texas and Virginia. Consequently, a war broke out between the North and the South, but contrary to popular belief, this war wasn't about ending slavery; it was more about the preservation of the United States as a nation. It was a fight against the secession. The Southern States, on the other hand, wanted to secede from the United States because they did not want to abolish slavery, so for them, the war was about slavery. For Abraham Lincoln, however, it was about stopping the secession. Of course, we all know what happened. The South lost, the Confederate States of America were never legitimized, and slavery was finally abolished in 1863 through the Emancipation Proclamation. Slavery ended in all American states, however, in December of 1865, it was officially abolished by the Thirteenth Amendment. Many of the slaves who were free in 1863 didn't get the news for two years, so they kept working under the oppressive thumbs of their masters. Vice.com reported, "Historian and genealogist Antoinette Harrell has uncovered cases of African Americans still living as slaves 100 years after the signing of the Emancipation Proclamation" (Source: Vice/Blacks Were Enslaved Well into the 1960s/Antoinette Harrell; as told to Justin Fornal). There were people still living and serving as slaves all the way up to the 1960's! Having been raised in Mississippi, I can't say that I am totally shocked because of the in-your-face racism that's still prevalent there today. Of course, people won't walk up to you and call you a derogatory name, but racism is interwoven into Mississippi's culture, for example, some restaurants still have their workers segregated. My mother worked part-time at a restaurant like that; the guy had all of his Black workers in the back cooking and washing dishes, but he had all of his White workers on the front, serving as cashiers and waitresses. The only White man in the back was the chef. Even when I was young, I would often confront my mother, telling her she needed to report them, but she'd always counter with, "If I said something, they'd fire me." When I would tell her that I was going to call around and see who to report the racism to, she would jokingly say, "You better not." And while she was laughing, I knew she was serious. Being treated like a second-class citizen was normal to her, and she was so passionate about making sure that her kids ate and had a roof over their heads that she just decided to accept it. Thankfully, that wasn't her main source of income; it was just a part-time job that she took to make ends meet, nevertheless, she still worked under those conditions. Like many Blacks from her generation, she was too afraid to come against a system of inequality and injustice, so-much-so that she accepted racism as a norm. Amazingly enough, slavery was not abolished in Mississippi until 2013! You read that right—2013! While no one owned any slaves (at least officially), the records show that Mississippi failed to do its part in abolishing slavery. ABC News reported the following, "Until February 7, 2013, the state of Mississippi had never submitted the required documentation to ratify the Thirteenth Amendment, meaning it never officially had abolished slavery" (Source: ABC News/Mississippi Officially Abolishes Slavery, Ratifies 13th Amendment/Ben Waldron). No wonder it is the poorest state in the Union! No wonder, despite the progression of every other American state, Mississippi has lagged behind in just about every arena! And anyone who knows the state of Mississippi knows that neglecting to sign the Thirteenth Amendment was not an oversight on our government's end, it was pure rebellion. This is reminiscent of when Christ freed us from the curse of the law. Many Jews refused (and still refuse) to accept Him, thus, denying themselves the salvation and the freedom He so lovingly extended to them.

All the same, many people today are still serving under the Mosaic Law, not realizing that they are now free from it. So, they're still wrestling with guilt, shame and condemnation, believing that if they beat themselves up, they will prove how sorry they are to God.

Despite Mississippi's in-your-face racist culture, I didn't experience as much direct racism as many of the people I know. I experienced more direct racism when I started working at Walmart at the age of 17. As a cashier, I would sometimes have people to refuse to put their money in my hand. These were almost always elderly White guys who looked to be around 70-years old or above. I didn't take too much offense to their behavior because I actually marveled at the fact that they had one leg in the grave and still wasn't afraid of God. Even though I wasn't saved, I feared God. One racially motivated incident that sticks out to me the most, however, took place a few years later when I was working in the lingerie department. The department was called lingerie, but we also covered the purses, backpacks, and gift items. One day, I was helping a man in a wheelchair when a woman walked up to me and shouted out, "Ma'am, can somebody help me?!" She was a middle-aged White woman with short brunette hair and very hateful eyes. "Yes ma'am. I'll be with you in a few minutes," I said in the most chipper way I could. "I'm helping someone else." I was helping a guy who was shopping for a gift for his mother, and because he was wheelchair bound, he could not reach some of the shelves. I was helping him to choose a gift by pulling down some of the gifts so he could look at them and I was making suggestions because he didn't know what to get her. He was also White, but unlike the woman, he was very kind. Maybe ten to fifteen minutes later, I heard my name being called. I turned around and saw one of my assistant managers walking in my direction with the woman alongside her, and she was furious! "Tiffany, did you tell this lady that you weren't going to help her?!" my manager shouted. I looked at the woman and then back at my manager before saying no. Before I could explain, the woman interjected, "Yes, you did!" I don't remember everything that she said, but she accused me of calling her out of her name and refusing to help her. I was taken aback. I couldn't believe that she was standing there, looking me in the eyes and lying on me. My manager started firing off at me, and the woman kept talking as well. She accused another woman I worked with of verbally attacking her and refusing to help her. That woman walked up and started defending herself as well. We were on the verge of losing our jobs and we knew this. We needed a miracle to take place because it was clear that our manager believed this woman and she was livid. Another co-worker walked up so that she could listen to everything that was going on, and when the woman saw her, she yelled out, "Her too!" Again, I don't remember all of the accusations she launched at us, but I do remember that particular co-worker's response. She laughed loudly and then calmly said, "Now, I know you're lying! I JUST clocked in!" And just like that, the woman's lies were exposed, but the icing on the cake came from the guy in the wheelchair. He was within earshot of the conversation, so he made his way over to us and said, "Ma'am, you know that that's not true. She was helping me when you walked up. All she said to you was that she'd be with you in a few minutes because she was helping someone else. She was very kind to you and very helpful to me. Please don't lie on this nice woman." Exposed and ashamed, the woman's face turned red. My manager then turned to look at her, and without saying another word, the woman suddenly stormed off. My manager apologized and we all stood around and discussed what had just taken place. The guy in the wheelchair stuck around for a few minutes as well and asked if he could fill out a card to talk about how helpful and kind I had been to him. He even apologized for that woman's behavior. This was the first time I'd experienced anything like that upfront and personal. My next face-to-face encounter took place when I was maybe 21-years old. Me and two of my co-workers had been sent to Louisiana to help out at another Walmart; I think this was in Shreveport. That particular store had been severely damaged in a fire, and they'd just finished repairing it. We went there to help restock and organize the ladies' department. The first red flag came after we arrived. When they saw us, a couple of the managers immediately said that we wouldn't be working our normal shifts (7am to 4pm); instead, we'd be working overnight. Of course, we weren't happy about this, so we called our store manager, but he told us to go ahead and comply since it was only for a week. There were people who'd traveled from other stores there to help as well, and we soon discovered that they did not tell the Whites to work overnight. Only the Blacks were given that shift. The assistant managers were clearly racist. They would not talk with us; instead, they would send the Black assistant to say whatever they wanted to say, but they didn't act like this with the White employees, and we all saw this. The Black employees seemed a little off to us. They were friendly, but they were clearly fearful; they appeared to be trained. This was not too surprising, given the fact that my mother had worked in a racist environment, so I'd seen this behavior before. I remember seeing a lady drop her head whenever one of the assistant managers came around; she would just answer her questions, but would not look her in the eyes.

We were supposed to be there one week, but we ended up staying two, maybe three days. This is because on the second or third night, one of the assistant managers came up to me and one of my co-workers. I think she had the same rank as the other assistant managers (I could be wrong), but she clearly didn't have the same power. Of course, she was Black. She was on the work-floor working just like the rest of us, while the two White assistants stood around, watching and talking amongst each other. They would walk around together like they were glued together at the hip, but this wasn't completely abnormal because in our home store, we had assistants like that. The Black assistant said to us, "Be very careful when y'all go to the bathroom. Try not to go so much and try not to go together. They've been complaining." She then went on to tell us that the two assistant managers had said that me and one of my co-workers had taken several bathroom breaks the night before, and we kept going to the bathroom together. They'd then told her to address us about this. The problem is that this was a blatant lie. We'd only gone to the bathroom one time, and this was on our break. While she was talking, I felt anger rising up in me. It was already clear to us that the women had a White supremacist mindset just by the way they treated us, and this was something I could ignore, but being lied on was not something I could look past. And what got me angrier was when she told me that the women kept referring to me and my co-worker as "them gals." While the woman was still warning us, I took off walking in the direction of the White assistants who were standing afar off. "Tiffany! Tiffany!" I could hear my name being called from behind, but I just kept walking until I reached the women who were, like always, standing together.

"Which one of you said that we kept going to the bathroom last night and the other night?"
(One of the women proudly raised her hand.)
"I did. I saw you two go to the bathroom at least three or four times together."
"Well, first off, I'm not 'a gal,' my name is Tiffany! And secondly, you're lying through your teeth! We went to the bathroom one time, and this was during our break! I don't know what you think you saw, but you did not see us!"
"No, I saw you clearly with my own two eyes. You went to the bathroom several times."

"Well, it sounds to me like you need your eyes
checked! You must've seen a ghost or something
because you did not see us! Maybe, all Black folks
look the same to you, but I know what I did and did
not do!"
*(By this time, a few workers had started gathering
around and that crowd slowly grew to around ten to
fifteen people).*
"You need to calm down. As a matter of fact, follow us
to the office."
"I'm not following you anywhere! Like I said, don't
reference me unless you're going to tell the truth!
We're here to help y'all out, not the other way around!
We went to the bathroom one time each night while
on our breaks, and we were in there maybe two
minutes each time, so I don't know why you took it
upon yourself to lie on us, but I'm not the one!"
"No, I … we clearly saw the both of you constantly
going in and out of the bathroom. This is something
we don't tolerate...."
"I don't know if all Black folks look the same to you,
but you did not see me or my friend going to the
bathroom outside of our break, so like I said, you
need to get your eyes examined and stop lying!"
(The other assistant jumped in.)
"Like she said, we saw you two going to the bathroom
on several occasions, so this is not up for discussion.
Follow us to the office right now!"
"And like I said, all Black folks don't look the same, so

you must've seen a ghost or you must've been high on something! I don't know how y'all do things around here, but I'm not about to stand here and let you lie on me! And I'm not going anywhere with you!"

"Follow us to the office—now!"

(Crosses arms.) "Make me!"

This is when one of the women I'd been traveling with broke through the crowd. She was maybe 35-years old, and if they thought I was outspoken, they were in for an earful. She yelled at the women, "She's not going anywhere with y'all!" I remember that she stepped in front of me, getting a few inches closer to them than I had been. In other words, she was in their personal space. "If she's going to the office, we are going to the office! They are with me! If she goes down, we all go down!" The women both started turning red. One of them spoke up, "No, we are just going to meet with her in the office and everyone else needs to go back to work." That's when my co-worker spoke up again. "Do you speak English?! She's with me! And if she goes to the office, we are ALL going to office! And everybody in this crowd knows y'all lying! They were out on this floor working their tails off like the rest of us, so I don't know what y'all got up your sleeves, but you got the right ones on today! I promise you that!" The other lady who'd traveled with us finally spoke up as well; she was the one I'd been accused of going to the bathroom with. "That's right! We're a team. If she goes to the office, we all go to the office! Like she said, we went to the bathroom one time each night, so I don't know why y'all lying." I remember looking around at the Black workers there and feeling like I'd stepped back into the 1920's. They were looking at us with fear in their eyes, and a few of them were even gesturing with their eyes for us to settle down. I genuinely could not believe what I was seeing. Needless to say, we did not follow those women to the office; instead, we left the store that night, and the next morning, we checked out of our hotel and went back to Mississippi. They were lying on us, but it didn't take us long to realize where they were heading with those lies. They were about to accuse us of theft, and neither of us had ever stolen anything from our store or that store. We weren't thieves; we were honestly three women who our store manager revered as his hardest and most trusted workers. That's why he'd sent us to help them out. Cathy, the woman who'd spoken up, was one of the hardest workers at our store, and she was the most celebrated, winning many awards for keeping her department organized. She was a department manager and her work ethic was extremely impressive. She appeared to be the quiet type; she rarely said much. She just went straight to work, and she was always very kind. But we all knew that she was outspoken when she needed to be. When I'd stood up to the assistants, I honestly did not expect anyone to back me up, but to see her stand up the way that she did gave me a new level of love and respect for her. She risked it all to make sure that I wasn't lied on. On the ride back to the hotel that night, she was the one who helped us to see the situation from another angle. At first, we thought they were lying on us because they were racist and wanted us to lose our jobs, but Cathy had another point of view. She said, "They were about to set y'all up. That's why I wasn't about to let you go into that office with them. I believe they are stealing from that store and they were looking for someone to take the fall. Y'all were about to become their scapegoats. If they had gotten you in that office, there's no telling what they were going to do to you." Cathy was passionate about her beliefs, and after talking about it, we all came to the same conclusion. After all, why would they tell an outright lie? Misunderstandings are a part of human life, but this was no misunderstanding. They were literally making up stories about us. Nevertheless, that day, we stood together in unity, so whatever they had up their sleeves was thwarted. And for anyone who feels like I should have just shrugged the accusation off and not confronted the women, you have to understand racism to fully grasp why I did what I did. A silent accusation from a White woman in the South was enough to destroy a Black person's career, name and even that person's life. And while I don't believe my life was in danger, my job was. You see, had I not said anything, they would have given that false report to my manager, and as a result, my employment could have been terminated. Then again, they were likely testing us before launching an accusation against us, so they set the stage for the lies they were about to tell. Nevertheless, I confronted them publicly about the lies that they were trying to utter privately. I learned a long time ago that what's unsaid is oftentimes more dangerous than what's said. In other words, if someone lies on you and you don't address that lie, it could potentially ruin your life.

Once we reentered Mississippi, we went to our home store to clock out and turn in our timecards (this was so that we could report all the hours that we'd worked in Louisiana). Of course, by then, our manager had already gotten wind of the situation. A tall White and somewhat muscular guy, he looked a lot like a redheaded version of Christopher Reeve. He knew how outspoken I could be when provoked, so he came directly to me. He had a slight smirk on his face as he watched me mess with the time clock. He leaned against the wall and said nothing for a few seconds. Finally, he spoke up. "Tiffany" he said calmly. *(Sigh)*. "What did you do—now? Tiffany, what did you say to those women?" he asked. I could hear his voice quivering as if he was trying to contain his laughter (or his anger). I was still somewhat angry about the event. "They lied and said that me and Tonia went to the bathroom four times in one night! I told them that all Black folks don't look alike, and if they saw two Black women going to the bathroom that looked like us, they must've seen a ghost! They got the right one, because ...." Before I could finish talking, he walked off chuckling and shaking his head. I couldn't tell if he found the situation humorous or if he was just trying to contain his anger. Cathy later told me that he found the situation humorous because he knew the risk involved with sending us down there; we were some of his hardest workers, but we were also some of his most passionate workers. He'd likely been in that particular Walmart before, so he knew what we'd be facing when we got there. Nevertheless, he decided to take the risk because we were all hard workers who honestly rarely took breaks. We didn't get into any trouble and life continued on as normal. I'm pretty sure the women thought that because we were from Mississippi that our store was just as racist and oppressive as theirs (if not more), but they were wrong. We didn't have racist managers, and if any of them were racist, we didn't know it.

The word I want to highlight in the aforementioned story is RISK! Change will never happen and can never happen until someone risks it all to come up against injustice and demonic systems were willing to comply with the demonic systems, and this made it all the more difficult for the folks who fought up against it. The Civil War saw 618,222 deaths—3. Moses was a risk-taker. Harriet Tubman was a risk-taker. No one has ever accomplished anything great without first having to face some Goliath-sized risks. The generation before me had some fighters in it, but there were too many passive people who 60,222 men who fought for the North lost their lives, while 258,000 from the South lost their lives. Anytime a new system is being implemented and an old system is being dismantled, you will almost always see bloodshed. This is the parting of the Red Sea between two seasons. I risked my job that day, but my risk wasn't as big of a sacrifice as Cathy's risk, after all, I was 20 or 21-years old, living at home with my mother. I could afford to be jobless, but she couldn't. She was around 35-years old and she was a single mother. Nevertheless, she saw injustice taking place and she stood in the gap for me and the other co-worker. This provoked the other co-worker to speak up. I believe that God sent us there to stop whatever foolishness those women had planned, because whatever it was, they would have likely done it to someone else. But because I confronted them out in the open, their plans were disrupted. All the same, God sent us there to give the other employees the courage they needed to speak up for themselves. While we were from one of the most racist states in the United States, we were also from a different generation than our parents. We'd counted the costs and we knew the risks involved with speaking up, and yet, we were willing to pay that price without hesitation. Again, the word I want to place emphasis on is the word "risk." What are you willing to risk to accomplish your goals and move out of the season you're in? Luke 6:38 says, "Give, and it shall be given unto you; good measure, pressed down, and shaken together, and running over, shall men give into your bosom. For with the same measure that ye mete withal it shall be measured to you again." You can't get something valuable without first giving up something valuable. If you give a little, expect to receive a little in return. And if God entrusts you with big gifts, He expects a big return on His investment. Luke 12:48 says it this way, "For unto whomsoever much is given, of him shall be much required: and to whom men have committed much, of him they will ask the more." In other words, change can be expensive, but you get to determine whether it's worth it to you or not. Oftentimes, when you're challenging a system, what you have to give up is your comfort. There are other times when you have to be willing to risk your life, especially when challenging a system built on or established by blood. Remember, we discussed earlier that a covenant is established by blood and can only be fulfilled, nullified or dismantled by blood. In other words, if a witch sacrifices her child to establish a demonic system, it will take blood to break that system. Thankfully, we now have the blood of Jesus to dismantle it, but this doesn't mean that there won't be any sacrifices on our ends. This is all the Big U (ultimatum) that we discussed earlier is about. The enemy will try to get you to place great value on things and people within a certain season, and all too often, when you're about to exit that season, he will hold those relationships and those things over your head. On that day or in that moment, you will know that if you take another step forward, your life is going to be drastically altered. The Israelites knew that the moment they stepped into the Red Sea, their lives would never be the same again.

Before you leave a season, you have to absolutely bankrupt that season. If you don't, the enemy will use whatever it is that you did not get to seduce you back into bondage. This is what the Israelites did before leaving Egypt. Exodus 12:36 reads, "And the LORD had given the people favor in the sight of the Egyptians, so that they let them have what they asked. Thus they plundered the Egyptians." This is why the Bible tells us not to chase riches. Our job is to simply overcome the mindsets that are enslaving us and to walk in the victory that Christ has afforded us through His shed blood. When we do this, we get to plunder the enemy! Remember, when the enemy is found, he has to restore seven-fold of what he's stolen! Get this—when the enemy has absolutely NOTHING left to offer you, you then become as powerful as you're designed and designated to be! In other words, if you're willing to forsake your own comforts, your own plans, your own desires and every opportunity that rises up, the enemy literally has no place in you! In other words, he has no power over you in any given state! Anytime you forsake a comfort zone, you will end up uncomfortable; that's a given. But are you willing to forsake your own comfort to see a change in your life, your family, your church, your community, your city or your country? Amazingly enough, most Christians are not. Many Christians have mastered the regions of thought they are in; this is why they are super emotional and religious. I teach a writer's class and I'm often shocked at what little fight some believers have in them. The minute they become uncomfortable or offended, they quit. But these are the same people who will swear on a Bible that God told them to write a book. They admire the finished projects of other authors; they envy the book signings, photo shoots and the extra streams of income that other authors get to enjoy, but that's just the front end of the process! Every system has a dashboard, and behind the scenes, there's oftentimes a lot of research, time invested, time lost, tears, financial losses, altered relationships and frustration put into building that system. Howbeit, if a believer isn't willing to be uncomfortable enough to finish a book, how can we expect that same Christian to fight against demonic systems? We can't! They'll pray and be emotional, but the minute the enemy ransacks their comfort zones, they'll start calling themselves Muslims or Five Percenters. In other words, they have made an idol out of comfort! This isn't new! There were slaves who were comfortable being slaves! They weren't willing to go up against their slave-owners or the systems put in place to keep them uneducated and dependent on their masters. Think about the exodus from Egypt that the Israelites took. Most of them would rather return to those demonic, oppressive systems than to be uncomfortable, but thankfully, Moses had been prepared for that event. He'd forsaken the comfort of the castle forty years prior to that. What's crazy is, confronting Pharaoh was child's play in comparison to his next season, and that was leading a bunch of bound, religious folks through the hallways of one season towards another. The hallway is often the most difficult part of a transition. Remember, it's the wilderness between two seasons or mindsets; it's the time allotted by God to deliver us from the residue of our last season. But all too often, we refuse to be fully purged, reasoning within ourselves that if we don't reach our promised lands, at least, we'd be able to return to our oppressors. And it is for this reason that the majority of believers don't start the businesses, create the inventions, finish the books or do anything that requires them to sacrifice their comfort. This is also why divorce is so prevalent; yes, even in the church. Just like all things, marriages have twists and turns! The person you are today isn't necessarily the person you'll be tomorrow; this is why you need a spouse who's flexible enough to let you grow, and secure enough to let you breathe. People who aren't secure enough to let their spouses grow will almost always let their spouses go; that is, if they refuse to settle down in mediocrity.

You are free. Your mind has to adjust to accept this truth. It doesn't matter who you are, what you've done, what you've been through or what color your skin is—Christ paid the ultimate price for you! And you don't need anyone's permission to be as blessed as you were created to be! You are no longer a slave unless you choose to be. And if you need evidence of your freedom, here are your papers:

Chapter/Verse	Scriptural Evidence of Your Freedom
John 3:17	"For God did not send His Son into the world to condemn the world, but that the world through Him might be saved."
Psalm 103:12	"As far as the east is from the west, so far has He removed our transgressions from us."
Romans 8:1	"There is therefore now no condemnation to those who are in Christ Jesus, who do not walk according to the flesh, but according to the Spirit."
2 Corinthians 5:17	Therefore, if anyone is in Christ, he is a new creation; old things have passed away; behold, all things have become new."

Chapter/Verse	Scriptural Evidence of Your Freedom
Ephesians 1:7	"In Him we have redemption through His blood, the forgiveness of sins, according to the riches of His grace."
Isaiah 1:18	"'Come now, and let us reason together,' says the Lord, 'Though your sins are like scarlet, they shall be as white as snow; though they are red like crimson, they shall be as wool.'"
1 John 1:19	"If we confess our sins, He is faithful and just to forgive us our sins and to cleanse us from all unrighteousness."
Hebrews 8:12	"For I will be merciful to their unrighteousness, and their sins and their lawless deeds I will remember no more."

It's important to note that while you are free, you can go out there and get yourself bound again. That's all temptation is about; it's centered around getting people back into Egypt (bondage). Jesus stopped the religious folks from condemning people who were caught in sin, of course, but He also told the sinner to repent. Consider the story of the woman caught in the act of adultery. He didn't look at her and say, "Child, you're good! Just try not to get caught next time because you know how religious folks can be..." No! Let's look at how He responded! John 8:2-11 tells the story this way, "And early in the morning he came again into the temple, and all the people came unto him; and he sat down, and taught them. And the scribes and Pharisees brought unto him a woman taken in adultery; and when they had set her in the midst, they said unto him, Teacher, this woman was taken in adultery, in the very act. Now Moses in the law commanded us, that such should be stoned: but what say you? This they said, testing him, that they might have to accuse him. But Jesus stooped down, and with his finger wrote on the ground, as though he heard them not. So when they continued asking him, he lifted himself up, and said unto them, He that is without sin among you, let him first cast a stone at her. And again he stooped down, and wrote on the ground. And they who heard it, being convicted by their own conscience, went out one by one, beginning at the eldest, even unto the last: and Jesus was left alone, and the woman standing before him. When Jesus had lifted himself up, and saw none but the woman, he said unto her, Woman, where are those your accusers? Has no man condemned you? She said, No man, Lord. And Jesus said unto her, Neither do I condemn you: go, and sin no more." In other words, He did not approve of what she'd done, just as He did not approve of how the scribes and Pharisees responded to what she'd done. He rebuked them ALL! Let's get something clear …

- Jesus paid the price for our sins, so if we have confessed with our mouths and believed in our hearts that He is Lord and that God raised Him from the dead, we are saved!
- We all fall short of God's glory—daily!
- The younger we are in the faith, the more we are prone to rebelling against God. This is why we need

grace! Grace is the space in any given season for us to realize, not what we did, but <u>why</u> we did it; this deals with how we think! It's the space to change our minds and mature! It is not a license to rebel! (See Revelation 2:18-22.)

- There is a blessing attached to "doing" the right thing, even when we're tempted to do otherwise! "And let us not be weary in <u>well doing</u>: for in due season we shall reap, if we faint not" (Galatians 6:9). In other words, I don't have to wait to understand why something is wrong if God told me not to do it; instead, I refrain from it, and then, understanding will meet me at the cross! Why? Because I didn't just settle with knowledge, I plowed until I got understanding!

- Rebellion is as the sin of witchcraft! Rebellion is knowing that something is wrong, but still doing it. And while we are no longer under the law of works, we are still commanded to manifest the works of faith! This is why the Bible says that faith without works is dead. Your works are the fruits of your belief system, and while you won't be condemned because of them, you can get yourself bound. Every deliverance minister knows the importance and the power of a decision! Please note that you won't get bound if you make a mistake; we all miss the mark! Bondage is usually the result of repeated rebellion or ignorance.

In other words, God has drawn a line in the sand. Honor those boundaries and be led by His Spirit. This is how you escape bondage and this is how you avoid being bound. And get this—I'm not someone who's telling you how to get free based on what somebody told me. Yes, I am a student of the Word, but I'm also a client—a walking miracle, a living testimony and proof of what God can do to a submitted soul! Every time I look back at how far I've come, my faith grows another inch. I legally escaped the strongmen that held my family in captivity generation after generation. Was it easy? No, it wasn't. Was it cheap? Not at all! I lost a lot of relationships on my journey because I kept advancing forward; I never allowed myself to be satisfied with a season enough to where I'd settle down in it or settle for it. I moved forward and I encouraged and still encourage everyone around me to do the same. I let the people who love being bound park in whatever season they chose to park in, and I forgive myself for not allowing false loyalty to make me think that I am obligated to park next to them. No, I encourage them, push them, pray for them, and if they insist on staying behind, I keep moving forward. My loyalty to God provokes me to chase His will for my life. We have to stop thinking that we are obligated to holding on to people who have obligated themselves to bondage; yes, even if they're related to us. Some of the most prolific boundaries you'll ever have to draw are in the Storge (familial) state. This is the state that you'll have to repeat yourself in the most; this is the state that you'll have to enforce your boundaries in the most. This is the state where you learn how to boldly face the world and the many bound folks that are in it. If you can't get your family to respect you, you won't be able to get anyone else to respect you. And please know that your family, your community and everyone who's familiar with you is going to find a way to label you. Don't be distracted by what they say; keep moving. For example, two of my relatives got together one day and told me that I was controlling. This was maybe ten years ago. Personally, I am repulsed by controlling people, so I wanted to know what would make them say this about me. I stood there and examined myself, but I could not think of one time I'd attempted to control them or anyone else. I realized that they had a shortage for labels, meaning, they were trying to describe a trait of mine that they did not like, but they didn't have the right words to explain, so they used what was already in their mental glossaries.

Understand that we all have a library of labels in our hearts, and if we've limited ourselves to our family members, our communities and the people we can relate to, chances are, we've misdiagnosed a LOT of people because of our lack of understanding. I was once guilty of this, but I opened up myself to people who didn't look or reason like me. So, I cross-examined my accusers. I asked them to:

1. Give me some examples of me trying to control them or anyone else.
2. Define the word "controlling."

Their examples and definitions proved once and for all that they were using the wrong label. They said that whenever my mind is made up about something, that I won't budge on that thing. Their stories were more than five years old, and even in those stories, they didn't describe a controlling woman, they described someone who was either stubborn or overzealous. They also described a woman who was intolerant. I brought this to their attention, describing what control is and letting them know that they were describing my zeal, my passion, and yes, sometimes, my ability to be stubborn. Howbeit, the reason this was problematic for them was only because my family was bound; they were used to fighting with each other and hurting one another until they got what they wanted. Nevertheless, I drew the line in front of this vengeful and abusive behavior. I closed every door in my life except the door of healthy communication. Anything else would not be tolerated. Anyone who wanted to be a part of my life had to use that door only. No other door was an option. To some people, this looks and feels like control, but it's not. It's called order. I can never tell a person what they have to do in their own personal lives; that's their business, but I set the stage for what's allowed and disallowed in my life. This may sound militant, but it works! It took years of me reiterating my boundaries, enforcing my boundaries and removing myself from toxic situations and people before they realized that I meant what I said. We had to discuss our differences and respect our differences; there was no room for anything else. Additionally, I established a zero-tolerance policy against vengeful behaviors, and I removed myself from anyone who violated that policy. Again, this may sound militant, but it worked! You see, I knew what I was dealing with in my family, and I knew that whatever I allowed in my life, Heaven also had to allow. I spoke with a relative of mine one day, and she told me that some of my other relatives were threatening to shoot up her car with her in it because they'd had a disagreement. This is the type of toxicity found in my family, and I do not tolerate it! Every person in your life will see a different side of you. I have family members who only see the loving, funny and helpful Tiffany; then again, there are family members who see a bunch of boundaries that they have to cross to get to me. This is because they are extremely toxic, and while I love them, I know that I have to put a fence between me and them—one that would stretch till the end of time if that's how long it takes them to change their minds. But this fence would allow me to communicate with them, love on them and be there for them, without giving them a seat in my life that they're not mature enough to handle. Think of it this way. If I owned a bank and I had a cousin who had been convicted five times of robbing banks, why would I then hire him to work for my bank UNLESS he'd become a new creature in Christ and I saw the fruit of this in his life? Hiring him just because he says that he's changed is like trying to spoon with an alligator and thinking that it'll appreciate you enough to not eat you; it's asinine! Consider the dream I spoke of about the freckled-faced demon and the fence. This is how some of your relationships need to look! There has to be a fence, a hedge, a boundary or a limitation between you and some of your family members, otherwise, they will rob you of your peace, your sanity and your future!

And if someone has been absent from my life for several years, I don't' let them just barge back in because I don't know them! They have to introduce or reintroduce themselves to me and meet the woman I am today. They can't just show up and think that I'm supposed to open my house and my life to them. I remember having a relative to reach out to me after 15 years of no contact, thinking that we were supposed to pick up where we left off. No! I like to take things slow! We have to build a new relationship and this takes time. She wanted to rush everything, but I wouldn't budge. By the end of that conversation, her true motives surfaced. She'd found out that I had a business and she wanted me to do some free work for her. I told her my prices and gave her a link to my website. When she started talking business, I put on my business hat. Again, this may sound harsh to some, especially if you come from a normal family, but for those of you who have come out of a toxic background, you truly have to be steadfast, unmovable and always abounding in the work of the Lord in regards to your boundaries. She reached out to me maybe two or three more times, but when she saw that I wasn't going to do the work for free, she never called or contacted me again. This is the power and the purpose of boundaries! The more I learned to walk in my God-granted authority, the more peace I had! I discovered gifts I didn't know I had when I was no longer distracted. Why? Because I plundered the Egyptians; that is, I took back what the enemy stole, not just from me, but from my family generations ago. And I'm still in the process of recovering it all.

No risk equals no gain. If your comfort is more important

than your purpose, your comfort will become your Egypt and you will become your own Pharaoh—or you will elect people to serve as Pharaohs in your life. Not everyone who has an oppressor is a victim; some of these oppressors are elected officials. Anyone who's done any measure of counseling or life-coaching can tell you this. There are people out there who surround themselves with abusive and controlling people, and one of their recreational activities is to set up counseling sessions just to talk about their oppressors. This is nothing but a mental vacation away from their narcissistic lovers or friends. But if you talk to them long enough, you'll come to see that they don't want help building their self-worth or removing themselves from those slave-quarters that they call relationships, they just want attention! You see, one of the traits of an oppressor is to punish his or her victims, for example, a narcissistic woman may decide that she's angry with her best friend because her best friend didn't answer her last two phone calls. Yes, there are people out there who are so emotionally wounded that they literally punish everyone in their lives for the silliest reasons. Anyhow, to teach her friend a lesson, she decides to not answer any of her calls for a week, and the one time she does answer her phone, she utilizes that moment to confirm her friend's fears. "I'm busy. I'll call you back," she snarls before hanging up the phone. Scared and confused, the oppressed friend tries to call her back to find out what's wrong. But the narcissist feels like she should automatically know what's wrong, so she leaves it up to her friend to figure it out. Unsettled, the friend sets up a counseling session, and when she finally meets with her coach or therapist, she talks nonstop about the many antics that her friend has pulled. The counselor interjects, "Ma'am, based on what you've told me, she's not your friend. She's your Pharaoh. You need to remove yourself from that relationship." The woman nods her head, and then continues on sharing story after story of the many abuses she's suffered at the hands of her narcissistic friend. The counselor repeats herself. "I hear you, but the solution to this is simple. That's not your friend. You need to cut all ties with that woman; you need to move on." After that, the woman acknowledges hearing what the counselor said with the nod of her head or by saying, "You're right," but then, she starts talking all the more about her friend's latest antics. In that moment, any coach or counselor worth their salt knows that the woman standing in front of them or on the other line of the phone does not want help. She just wants someone to talk to. In other words, she's relieving herself. Her Pharaoh is an elected official in her life, and she's not willing to dethrone that entity. They have a toxic co-dependency on one another. And this, of course, isn't limited to friends! I have seen more mother/daughter relationships like this than anything. All too often, the daughter will complain about her narcissistic, controlling and manipulative mother, but will not take any advice that requires her to come outside of her comfort zone in regards to her mother. If you tell her to set boundaries, she won't listen or she'll take what she wants from the advice and fashion it as a weapon against her mother. In other words, she's learned how to be as divisive as her mother. For example, if you tell her that she needs to cut ties with her mother or establish boundaries with her mother, she'll go back and say to her, "My counselor told me that I need to cut your behind off anyway! I don't even know why I'm still sitting here taking all this crap off of you! But just keep on! Your day is coming!" This is a ploy to scare her mother into submission. This is a wrestling match for power between two bound people. She took what the counselor told her and used it to gain leverage in an argument. This is actually pretty common, and if she doesn't get healed and delivered, she'll become just as divisive and narcissistic as her mother or even worse.

Again, no risk equals no gain. If you want to be everything that God has designed you to be, you have to get comfortable with being uncomfortable. This means that you have to take some risks! All the same, you have to hold your peace in those moments when it looks and feels like God has forsaken you, because He hasn't! It is during these times that He's pulling on what He's already invested in you! It is also during these times that He begins to reveal the hearts of the people around you. For example, let's say that you're going to college to become a lawyer. There are some people who will connect with you just because they want to be surrounded by powerful people. These are what we call power moves; this has nothing to do with them liking or even agreeing with you. I've seen people mistreat the folks at the entrance or bottom of a season, but kiss up behind folks who are just like the people they have disregarded! The people they are kissing up behind all have something in common—power, money and/or influence! These are power moves. Experience has taught me that at the end or peak of every season, just before you exit that region of thought, God will disconnect every person who's connected to you just to add you to their portfolios! This is because they've objectified you. In other words, they don't love you; their connection to you is "strictly business." And while this would be good if they connected with you in the right state and they'd honored you by paying for your services, they instead chose to go through the Philia state to get what they wanted from you. In other words, the enemy will use these people to advance into your life. Google defines "objectification" as "the action of degrading someone to the status of a mere object." This is the very thing that fuels serial killers, and people are using this fuel to build relationships with folks they don't like! This is both dangerous and ungodly, and it is for this reason that right before God graduates you to your next season, He begins to shake up your life so that any and everyone who has ill-motives will begin to manifest their intentions. One of God's most effective cleaning agents is called lowliness or humility. This is when God brings you low so that He can hide you. In other words, if you don't humble yourself, God will humble you, and when this happens, you will appear to be going nowhere to the people in your life. It will appear as if you've climaxed or given up. Every person who loves you will begin to encourage you, stand in the gap for you, correct you when you're off and pull on your potential. The people who connected with you because they were making power moves will wait a few months for you to recover because they fear that the moment they get up from that slot machine (you), someone else will come along and reap the benefits. But God will let them sit there until they have nothing left to give, and they will suddenly get up and exit your life—sometimes dramatically; at other times, they'll try to leave quietly. In other words, they'll stop calling and coming around, but they'll try to check in on you every now and again. Once you tell Lot where to go, God will speak to you and give you your next set of instructions. He'll take you into the hallway of your next season and begin to deliver you from all of the residue you picked up in your last region of thought. This time or space confirms to them that you aren't going anywhere, so anyone who's connected to you for the wrong reason will finally make their last appearances in your life; they'll go ahead and close the door between you and themselves if you haven't already closed it. Once this door is shut and you've been cleaned up, God will deliver you into your next season. This way, should the folks from your former season try to reemerge in your life, you will be fully aware of their intentions. Another cleaning agent He uses is called connections! God will allow the power-movers in your life to meet and connect with one of two types of people:

1. **People who they think are more powerful than you are**—BUT here's the kicker. The people they are connecting with won't be a fan of yours or won't be connected to you in any way. You see, people who make power-moves want to connect to as many powerful people as possible, so they wouldn't close the door between you and themselves unless there

was some incentive to do so. This incentive often comes in the form of people who look like they're going further than you, have more influence than you, have more money than you or have more power than you. In order to prove themselves to the new folks in their sights, these people will dramatically disconnect from you or do something to let you know that they are no longer affiliating themselves with you. This is called an OFFERING! What they're doing is killing their relationship with you so that they can have something of significant size to offer to their new connection! And get this—it will appear to work for a season! Their new connections will accept their offerings and sometimes even bring them close, but this has NOTHING to do with them; their newfound friends really want to know about you! What are your secrets, what are your weaknesses, what are your strengths, etc. In other words, they will find themselves being used in the same manner in which they attempted to use you! And by the time they realize they've been taken advantage of, it'll be too late! Their newfound friends will not trust them because of how they handled you and they'll find themselves wanting to reconnect with you. God may allow them to reenter your life, but they will never hold the same power or influence that they once held; that is, unless they truly humble themselves and stop chasing power!

2. **Insignificant others.** Most power-movers want so

badly to be in a relationship that they'll throw everyone in their lives away, including their children, for the opportunity to be some man's wife or some woman's husband. This is especially true if they meet someone who appears to be powerful or, at minimum, trainable. God will often allow them to meet what they believe to be the perfect Bonnie or Clyde, and from there, they'll focus all of their attention on these people. This is normal, however, they will oftentimes make a dramatic exit from your life because they don't think they need you anymore. They think that they are about to become your competition, so they have to create some type of rift between the two of you.

The point is, every time you're about to exit a season or go through an exodus, God will remove the people who cannot legally come with you. Sometimes, you won't be surprised when you see the people who fall away, and at other times, you'll be completely taken by surprise. As I mentioned earlier, I stepped into a church on a Friday night; this was before I found my tribe, and I was looking for a word from God. I was under an intense spiritual attack and I was trying to come out of it. The woman asked me to stand and told me that God was about to remove some people from my life who meant me no good. I knew who she was talking about. A year later, I walked into my God-assigned church for the first time, and the first prophetic word I got was, "God's about to remove some people from your life because they don't mean you any good." In other words, God repeatedly performed an enema on my life, and while it hurt, I welcomed it because I want everything that He has in store for me. And I don't just want the stuff, I want the call on my life; that's not for sale. So, I have been through a few exoduses, but I'm grateful for every last one of them. I didn't leave people behind; I left a mindset behind, and the folks that were attached to that mindset could not go any further with me.

We were on two sides of the same street.

If you've read Book Three, you are familiar with a dream I had of a guy who I'd allowed in my home, but without warning, I'd had a change of heart and asked him to leave. He refused to leave so I tricked him into leaving. I asked him to walk to the store with me, and he agreed. When we were walking, I noticed that he was on the same road in a different dimension. I could see him afar off, but there was a huge gulf dividing us. This gulf looked like a deep, dark and wide pit; it was impossible for him to cross over to where I was, and it was impossible for me to cross over to where he was, and I somehow knew this. As I mentioned in that particular book, that guy represented a devil. He represented something I'd once wrestled with. What's interesting is, the minute I got him out of my house, he lost all physical access to me. Howbeit, since I could hear him and he could hear me, he clearly still had enough access to where he could speak to me or at me. This voice is what we call temptation. Temptation, according to Dictionary.com, is "something that tempts, entices, or allures." It means to be lured by something or someone. Whatever lures you is a form of bait, and whatever or whoever is luring you either wants to devour you or use you as bait. Either way, you'd be consumed in the process. God can deliver you from everything that's unlike Him, but the voice of temptation will be around as long as there is breath in your body. But that's not the point I want to make, I want you to understand that some of the people in your life will have as much access to you as that demon had to me once I got him out of my house. You can see them, you can hear them, but they have to lose all intimate access to you if you want to cross over into your next season. What this means is that they can't be your best friends anymore or you close relatives; you have to treat them like Lot—in other words, you have to love them from a distance. You have to let them go in the direction they choose to go in while you continue to follow the voice of God. And like Abraham, if you discover that the enemy is attacking them, you should get the intercessors together to intercede on their behalves, but you shouldn't bring them back on your journey with you and don't go and sit in perversion with them. In other words, you have to forgive them, love them, pray for them, but change the password to your heart so they can no longer get in.

Please note that every season is preceded by a sea, and every sea is split by a decision. That is the personal decision that we make to walk out of bondage and into the hallways of our next seasons. This decision is called obedience! Before that sea splits, you have to make the personal decision that you are willing to lose whatever you have to lose to go wherever you have to go; this way, you can become who God designed you to be. This is what causes that hallway between your now season and your next season to open up, and this is what constructively evicts every Pharaoh operating in your life from whatever throne it's been sitting on. And please note that once God opens the door between your now season and your next season, you have to be willing to walk through it—immediately. This sounds easy, and most people will readily declare that they'd charge forward, but in truth, when they see what and who they're leaving behind, most people will go into passive rebellion. What is passive rebellion? One word—procrastination. It's telling God that you will do what He told you to do, but in your timing. This is similar to when your parents told you to go and wash the dishes, but you were playing the video game, so you said, "Give me a minute!" You used the element of time and the promise of compliance in your attempt to pacify your parents. Three hours later, your parents found you still glued to that game and the dishes still hadn't been washed. And when they said something about it, you once again proclaimed, "Okay! One minute! I'm coming!" In the middle of the night, your parents woke up to find you sound asleep, and the dishes still hadn't been washed. Of course, they woke you up and made you go and wash those dishes, and even then, you complained before complying. This is an example of passive rebellion. In other words, there's something in Egypt that you're still being entertained by. One thing my pastor always says is, "Everything that God does demands a response" (Apostle Bryan Meadows). In other words, if your Red Sea hasn't split yet and your Moses hasn't gone forward yet, this has NOTHING to do with time; it has EVERYTHING to do with your compliance to God's instructions. The Word tells us that obedience is better than sacrifice; we all know and agree with this. However, please know that delayed obedience is still disobedience. In other words, if you're procrastinating or still being entertained by something in Egypt, you are doing like many of the American slaves did once they got the news that they were free—they stayed behind and struck up a deal with their masters!

GENERATIONAL CURSES

The New York Times reported the following, "From Ur, Abraham traveled 700 miles to the borders of present-day Iraq, another 700 miles into Syria, another 800 down to Egypt by the inland road, and then back into Canaan - what is now Israel" (Source: The New York Times/Footsteps of Abraham/Malachi Martin). This journey was symbolic of the journey we would take as we walked out of the mindsets, the systems and the perversions of our forefathers.

Take a moment to read this article about a man named Mannix Franklin, his son and his grandson. This article was posted on the Milwaukee Journal Sentinel's website.

Infant, His Father and His Grandfather: Lives Cut Short

It is an unwelcome legacy:
Mannix Franklin Sr. was shot to death by Milwaukee police in 2003.
His son, Mannix Franklin Jr., was shot to death while visiting his mother in 2016.
And now, Franklin Jr.'s son, Mannix Franklin III, an infant, was found dead early Wednesday while sharing a sofa bed with his mother.

Franklin Sr.'s death on Halloween night 2003 made national headlines. According to testimony given at an inquest, Marnice Franklin called 911 about 8:30 p.m. and told the dispatcher that her 31-year-old husband, Franklin Sr., was harassing her in violation of a no-contact order. Among the officers who arrived at her home in 7900 block of W. Fond du Lac Avenue was Michael Pendergast, a two-year member of the department. Pendergast found Franklin Sr. hiding on a neighbor's driveway, witnesses said. Franklin Sr. began to walk toward Pendergast, his hand inside his jacket. Pendergast, his weapon drawn, ordered Franklin Sr. to stop and show his hands. Franklin Sr. refused to obey, Pendergast testified. Instead, he continued to walk toward the officer, pulling at something in his jacket. Pendergast shot him five times. On June 3, 2004, a six-member inquest jury deliberated nearly four hours before recommending charges not be filed.

Franklin Sr.'s son's death on Sept. 12, 2016, created less of a stir. It was a local story. Mannix Franklin Jr., according to court records, was shot to death while he was visiting his mother at her apartment in the Village of Brown Deer. His mother's 61-year-old friend, Jessie James, told police he killed Franklin Jr. with a single shot from his 12-gauge shotgun because the 22-year-old was talking back and being disrespectful. According to electronic records, James pleaded guilty in December to second-degree reckless homicide. He was sentenced to 20 years in prison and 10 years of extended supervision.

If his son's death made a stir, no one heard it.

The body of Mannix Franklin III — born on New Year's Day — was found beside his sleeping 21-year-old mother about 4 a.m. Wednesday, according to a Milwaukee County medical examiner's report. The infant and his mother had slept together on a fold-out sofa in the small one-bedroom apartment they shared with Mannix III's great-great-grandmother, the report says.

Family members mourned at the apartment Thursday night. They had drawn the drapes closed, and dark as it was, they turned on but a few lights. "Too much sadness," the mother said. "I'm still grieving for his dad," she said. "It feels like everything is being taken away so fast."

(Source: Milwaukee Journal Sentinel/ Infant, his father and his grandfather: Lives cut short/Crocker Spencer)

The man in question was my uncle. He was my mother's youngest brother. His name and his legacy were wiped completely off the face of the Earth. One of his older brothers (Elton Franklin) had been killed in a house fire just a few years prior to this. Amazingly enough, he'd managed to save his son before collapsing to the ground, according to a few witnesses. He'd run out of the house with his three-year old son in his hands, threw his son at the paramedics and then collapsed. He was covered with fire so much so that they couldn't see his face. Nevertheless, he ran out of his house holding his son. He then tossed his son towards the paramedics before collapsing. If it were up to the enemy, his son would have died in that fire. Instead, he received burns on one side of his face. What was this all about? This was a generational curse! Now, I can't say what my grandparents, great-grandparents or ancestors did while they were on the face of this Earth, but just looking at the issues that plagued my family (perversion, rebellion, idolatry, rage, hatred, murder, divorce, mental illness and a host of other issues), I can pretty much take a wild guess. Chances are, someone along the way thought it was a good idea to play with witchcraft. And they didn't just play with it, they obviously gave themselves over to it. And when witchcraft is in a family, it will normally manifest itself generation after generation until it is finally confronted and abolished. I remember my mother bringing home a Ouija board when I was around 15-years old. We had that Ouija board for a few months before my brother and I took it outside and ripped it in half (without my mother's knowledge, of course). We did this because our house had become extremely chaotic. Everything was going downhill, including our parents' marriage. They'd argued a lot over the course of our lives, but during this era, they could barely stand in the same room together without getting into a heated argument. Those arguments often turned into physical fights with my mother attacking my dad, my brother and I hiding all of the knives, and my dad calling the cops.

One day, a woman came over to our house so that my dad could do her taxes. She appeared to be in her mid to late sixties or early seventies, and she was dressed like a nun.

I'm not sure what her religious background was, but the outfit she wore was gray. I remember her sitting on the couch calmly waiting on my dad to come out of the backroom. If I remember correctly, my parents were arguing. I was drawn to the woman and so was my brother. I told the woman that my parents had been fighting a lot lately, and I will never forget what she said. She looked at the Ouija board on the table, pointed at it and said, "That's why." She then explained to my brother and myself that the Ouija board was a way of communicating, not with the dead, but with the devil. We were baffled. My brother and I turned and looked at one another with fear in our eyes. She told us that if we wanted the devil to get out of our house, we needed to get rid of that Ouija board. We nodded our heads in agreement and began to come up with a plan, after all, my mother had been the one who'd purchased the board. We had to find a way to make it disappear without her noticing that it was gone. We reasoned with one another that we could not tell our mother because she would not have believed the woman, so the "devil's board" would have remained in our small apartment. So, we plotted on how to get rid of the board. I don't know who told us that throwing the Bible on the Ouija board would make it go up in flames, but I do remember us taking the Ouija board outside and throwing it on the grass. We stood far away and threw the Bible at the Ouija board (I'm almost ashamed to admit this now). When it finally landed on the Ouija board, nothing happened. Our innocence and ignorance might have caused all of Heaven and hell to laugh at us, but we were determined to get the devil out of our

135

house. Even though the Ouija board had not caught on fire like we thought it would, we were both still afraid to approach it, thinking that it would suddenly combust once we got closer to it. Obviously, we had watched one too many scary movies. I finally got up enough gut to walk over and kick the board. I then picked up the Bible and took it in the house. Next, I returned and picked up the Ouija board, and my brother and I agreed to rip it in half. He grabbed one side of it, and I held onto the other side. We pulled that board (in opposite directions) with all of our might until it finally ripped. We then placed it in the community trash can, because we didn't want our mother to find it. Why did my mother feel the need to purchase a Ouija board? It was witchcraft manifesting in our bloodline! My mother simply didn't know any better, and my dad would just go along with her, even though he'd been brought up in church. Now, don't get me wrong—my mother wasn't an aggressive, loud or controlling woman. She was actually very docile, mild-mannered and meek. However, like my dad, she was battling with her own generational strongholds.

Generational curses are the result of spiritual lines being crossed generations ago. And you will see each generation crossing those same lines until someone wakes up and wholeheartedly repents. This means that the person in question will return to God, not just in confession, but indeed (faith without works is dead). That person will renounce the works of the enemy, and then, denounce the works of the enemy.

Renounce:

- to give up, refuse, or resign usually by formal declaration
- to refuse to follow, obey, or recognize any further

Denounce:

- to pronounce especially publicly to be blameworthy or evil
- to announce formally the termination of (something, such as a treaty)

(Both definitions were taken from Merriam-Webster).

I want you to imagine your family all grouped up and walking downhill. They are all walking in one direction, and they've been heading in this direction for centuries. But one day, you get tired of heading in that direction. You have your headset on, listening to the Bible and listening to your pastor preach the Word of God. Most of the folks in your family have pastors, but some of those pastors are heading in the same direction as your family! Finally, you've had it! You turn around and switch directions in an event called repentance. Now, you are heading uphill and dealing with the opposition that comes from your body (because it's not accustomed to ascending), along with the opposition from your family (these are the contrary winds that blow up against you as you ascend). They say that you're crazy, you are high-minded, you're mean, you're controlling—they say a lot of bad things about you! Some of your family members repent, but generation after generation, they've turned back around because they got tired of dealing with the weight, the pressure and the opposition coming from their loved ones. They stood to lose a lot, and they weren't willing to pay the cost associated with freedom. Instead, like zombies, they chanted religious quotes and kept heading downhill. "Only God can judge me," they shout repeatedly. "Let him who is without sin cast the first stone," they say as they continue downhill. And now, it's your turn. You are now going against the grain and it hurts! The worst part is, you feel absolutely alone in this! Everyone in your family is upset with you or expecting you to fall so they can laugh at you. You look up and see people at the top of the mountain eating and celebrating with their families. They are all Christians and they all seem to be happy, but when you look around, your family is divided by sin and religion. The only time you all come together is during holidays and at funerals because you cannot get along. Satan has divided your family so much so that you truly feel like you don't have a family. You have no one to call whenever you need encouragement. Sure, you could call your relatives and get a lot of bad advice, but you can't call them and talk too much about Jesus. So, you have a decision to make. Either you can ascend without your family, and be truly alone or you can descend (and argue) with them.

Matthew 10:37: He that loveth father or mother more than me is not worthy of me: and he that loveth son or daughter more than me is not worthy of me.

Matthew 12:47-50: Then one said unto him, Behold, thy

138

mother and thy brethren stand without, desiring to speak with thee. But he answered and said unto him that told him, Who is my mother? and who are my brethren? And he stretched forth his hand toward his disciples, and said, Behold my mother and my brethren! For whosoever shall do the will of my Father which is in heaven, the same is my brother, and sister, and mother.

If this is your story, you are not alone. What you are witnessing, experiencing and facing is a unique opportunity to change the direction of your family. You have been chosen, selected or even called to break the witchcraft off your family, and this is no easy charge. It makes me think about what I'd witnessed while living in Florida. I lived upstairs in an apartment that faced a large, man-made lake. I had a sliding door in my living room that led to the patio, so everyday, I would open the vertical blinds to let the natural sunlight come in. After that, I would work at my computer, but I would escape the work ever-so-often to look out at the lake. It was filled with all types of wildlife. I remember seeing a family of ducks swimming. There was one duck at the front, followed by another set of ducks that were being followed by another set of ducks. They were in a v-format as they swam. One duck at the very back of the formation immediately caught my attention because of how antsy he was. (Yes, it was a male duck. I knew this because of his coloration.) Anyhow, he seemed undecided. He'd swim behind the group, and then switch up a little. He'd swim out of formation, and then back in formation. Eventually, he made a decision.

Without warning, he turned around and started heading in the opposite direction. This immediately caught the attention of the ducks at the very back of the line; these were the ones that were nearest to him. All of a sudden, one of those ducks turned around and started following him, followed by another duck, and then another duck. Before long, the duck that had been at the very back was now leading the group, and the duck that had once been leading was now at the very back. Immediately, God used that opportunity to minister to me. He reminded me of Matthew 20:16, which reads, "So the last shall be first, and the first last: for many be called, but few chosen."

What I'd witnessed with the ducks was a picture of repentance and leadership. Sometimes, the matriarchs and patriarchs of a family are so broken, bound, jezebellic and corrupt that it will take an antsy millennial or someone from Gen-Z to suddenly turn around (repent) and just start following God, knowing full well that this could mean he or she may end up being outcast from the family. It goes without saying that anyone, regardless of what generation you're a part of, can break generational curses. The beautiful and blessed reward is that some people in that family will also turn around; this is how curses are broken! Someone has to be willing to count the costs and pay the price associated with going against the norm of his or her family! And believe me when I say, the witch, the warlock, the narcissist or the person acting as the strongman of that family will try to bring everyone back under his or her control.

That person will use the apaths (flying monkeys) of the family to harass, condescend and punish you for suddenly switching directions. Nevertheless, if you are the curse-breaker in your family, you can't be swayed by that person or his/her antics! You can't allow him or her to intimidate, manipulate or castigate you! There are things your family hasn't been able to do, places they've been unable to go and blessings they haven't been able to reach because of those familial strongholds, and they aren't going to go away on their own. If you don't break the curse, your children will have to wrestle with those devils. Believe it or not, Satan has plans for every family, but it takes someone who's more diligent, more persistent and more determined than he is to free a family from his crutches. For example, I had to look at my family and ask a whole lot of questions.

1. Why were we broke?
2. Why was perversion commonplace in our family?
3. Why was divorce prevalent in our family?
4. Despite how intelligent we were, why wasn't there anyone succeeding in my family, and for the ones who did tap into a measure of success, why did they literally run for their lives away from the family? Did they truly think they were better, or was there something more sinister taking place?
5. Why was just about everyone on welfare, and for the ones who aren't, why were they ostracized; that is, unless they were doing something illegal?
6. Why couldn't we come together as a family without someone starting a fight?

7. Why were there so many alcoholics, drug dealers and addicts in my family?
8. Why were the men dying at alarming rates?
9. Why was high blood pressure, diabetes and a host of other ailments plaguing my family?
10. Why did my family hate, but tolerate one another?

Enough! I finally started drawing a boundary around my peace when I was 15-years old. I think this was largely because I had friends whose families had taken me under their wings, and I was able to sit at dinner tables in peace. I started realizing that what I had been experiencing with my family was not normal after all! My friends became my family, and this wasn't because I didn't love my family. I love them wholeheartedly! I just realized that they (me included) had a LOT of healing to do, and there was no way I'd be able to heal if I kept going around them. I didn't just draw boundaries around myself, I broke up with the generational curse that had claimed the life of my uncles! I looked at the older women in my family and asked myself a life-altering question; that is, do I want their results? The answer was a resounding no! If you don't want your family's results, you have to do something different! In every bound family, someone has to finally say, "Enough is enough!" Someone has to offend the family by refusing to descend with them; that person has to ascend and pray their way through every wind of opposition that will blow their way! And please understand that I'm not telling you to intentionally go out and offend your family. What I am saying is that your choice to change directions will be looked upon by some as offensive! Like the ducks on the lake, when one person goes against the grain, others will eventually follow suit. Generational curses are broken when someone decides to not just ask for a blessing, but when he or she decides to become a blessing! Can you imagine the head-space that Abram was in when he had to leave behind his family and their religious practices? Can you imagine how frustrating and painful it was for David to know that his son, Absalom, did not value his life? Can you imagine the pain that Noah felt when he realized that his son, Ham, had tried to expose and humiliate him? The point is, you're not the only one with family problems. Nevertheless, you get to decide whether or not you'll be the curse-breaker in your family or if you'll leave it up to the next generation to fight or be conquered by the devils that you learned to live with.

GENERATIONAL BLESSINGS

I was doing a live video one day when the Lord started impressing it upon my heart to talk about generational blessings. What He said to me and through me not only changed the listeners' lives, but it changed my life as well. He said that there are blessings and answered prayers over many people that have been circling over their families' heads for generations, but no one has had the faith to pull them down. To me, they almost looked like birds flying over the heads of the people. For example, your great-grandparents may have been prophesied to that they were going to receive land that had been stolen from your family, wealth that had been held up by the enemy and peace on every side. But what they didn't realize was that anytime a prophetic word is released, the enemy comes behind it to bring doubt and confusion. What's amazing is he understands that he cannot stop that word from coming to pass because it is impossible for God to tell a lie! And since he can't stop it from coming to pass, his attack is designed to delay it. But before we go any further, let's look at a few scriptures.

Daniel 10:10-14: And, behold, an hand touched me, which set me upon my knees and upon the palms of my hands. And he said unto me, O Daniel, a man greatly beloved, understand the words that I speak unto thee, and stand

145

upright: for unto thee am I now sent. And when he had spoken this word unto me, I stood trembling. Then said he unto me, Fear not, Daniel: for from the first day that thou didst set thine heart to understand, and to chasten thyself before thy God, thy words were heard, and I am come for thy words. <u>But the prince of the kingdom of Persia withstood me one and twenty days</u>: but, lo, Michael, one of the chief princes, came to help me; and I remained there with the kings of Persia. Now I am come to make thee understand what shall befall thy people in the latter days: for yet the vision is for many days.

Mark 4:13-20: And he said unto them, Know ye not this parable? And how then will ye know all parables? The sower soweth the word. And these are they by the way side, where the word is sown; but when they have heard, Satan cometh immediately, and taketh away the word that was sown in their hearts. And these are they likewise which are sown on stony ground; who, when they have heard the word, immediately receive it with gladness; and have no root in themselves, and so endure but for a time: afterward, when affliction or <u>persecution ariseth for the word's sake</u>, immediately they are offended. And these are they which are sown among thorns; such as hear the word, and the cares of this world, and the deceitfulness of riches, and the lusts of other things entering in, choke the word, and it becometh unfruitful. And these are they which are sown on good ground; such as hear the word, and receive it, and bring forth fruit, some thirtyfold, some sixty, and some an hundred.

What? Did you think the prophetic word you'd received was a lie simply because it hasn't yet manifested for you? There is a possibility that it was an authentic word (you have the responsibility of testing the spirit and praying that word through if it is found to be sound). The minute a prophetic word is released over you, Satan is going to come for that word! Again, he can't truly "steal" it, but he can snatch it and hold it over your head (authority). What does this mean? It means that you'll have to repent and grow to reach it! You'll have to mature! He'll do this by attacking anything and everyone who is set in place to bring that word to pass in your life. Either that, or he'll attack your relationship with that person. For example, I can't tell you how many people have told me that upon meeting me, they initially hated me. One woman even told me that when she'd heard my voice for the first time, she couldn't stand the sound of it. Nevertheless, this was all demonic. Most of them eventually ended up on a call with me, going through deliverance. This is why I'm not alarmed when people are standoffish with me, especially in a spiritual setting like church. I know that, in many cases, it's not personal, it's spiritual. You see, whenever you ask God for something, He often sends a person to you or He sends you to a person. So, if you ask God for a husband, chances are, He will send a mentor to prepare the way for your husband. But the mentor may not necessarily be the type of mentor you want or maybe you don't see the need for mentorship. Here are a few common reasons that you may find yourself rejecting the mentor God has specifically and strategically chosen for you.

1. **You have commitment issues so you hate schedules.** Most people avoid mentorship because they have never remained faithful to anything that wasn't paying them. Because they are transactional in their thinking, they have trouble seeing the value of mentorship, so the only way they'd get a mentor is if someone paid them to do so. Since this just will not and does not happen, they embrace mediocrity. If a mentor does offer them some type of incentive for taking a mentorship class, most of them will not finish the course. Again, this is because they hate schedules and don't see the value in the concept of mentorship.

2. **The mentor doesn't look the way you want or expected him/her to look.** This is normally an issue for people in their twenties, all the way up to their mid-thirties. A woman who, for example, likes camouflage, combat boots and guns would likely reject mentorship from a woman who likes makeup, stilettos and hair extensions, and vice versa. This is because both women have a misconception or misguided belief about women who are unlike themselves. But when God sends a mentor your way, sometimes, He hides them behind exteriors that you wouldn't ordinarily embrace. Because you see specific personalities as "lower," God will usually hide your blessings behind those personality types; this way, you have to lower or, better yet, humble yourself to get to them!

3. **The mentor doesn't have the life or lifestyle that**

you want for yourself. This one is a double-edged sword of sorts because on one hand, you shouldn't take instructions from a person who doesn't have the results you want. However, your plans for you are not always God's plans for you. This is why you should pray about everyone; this way, you don't reject or delay the answer to your prayers. For example, I'm a two-time divorcee. I married both times when I was broken, immature, ignorant and bound. I was seriously bound! But those failed relationships did not disqualify me from teaching; they are actually the catalysts that God used to bring me to my knees! And now, He uses me to mentor and minister to Christian women, both married and unmarried. Howbeit, there are people who would refuse counsel from me (understandably) in favor of a woman who, for example, is happily married—a woman who did things right the first time. And she may be great and blessed, but this can and does serve as a snare for some women because the woman in question does not and has never struggled with the strongholds that they've struggled with, but I have. Maybe, she didn't come from a broken, narcissistic and toxic family, so she didn't attract narcissistic people to her. She can't relate to them, and because of this, it is hard for her to truly minister to their brokenness. Get this—she has her people; there are people specifically called to her because their histories match her history. Then again, there are women called to women like myself

149

because their histories match my history, and my job is to show them the mistakes I made, the beliefs I had and the lies Satan told me. My job is to also show them the revelation God shared with me as I began to ascend out of the pits that my family once called home. This is why most women who truly follow me are able to commit to abstinence, truly turn their hearts (and lives) around, get deliverance and understand/navigate the storms that they find themselves in as they ascend.

4. **You've heard rumors about the mentor.** People underestimate how strategic Satan is! Let's revisit the story that I told in Book Three about my friend, Asia. My other friends did not like her at all! They would roll their eyes at her and call her fake; that is, until Asia and I became friends. If you don't know the story, I used to hang around a group of girls at my former workplace. Asia also worked there. My clique of friends didn't like Asia because of how "prissy" she was. Nevertheless, Asia and I eventually became good friends. That's when I discovered that their misconceptions about her were false and assumed, and of course, I told them this. Thankfully, I wasn't swayed when they complained about me befriending everyone. I had my own mind, and this is what allowed me to become the woman I am today. They eventually got to know her a little more (they never truly became friends), and they came to realize that she wasn't the person they thought she was. Rumors

and misguided beliefs are nothing but Satan's way of intercepting your blessing the same way he intercepted the answer to Daniel's prayer!

5. **The people you like do not like your mentor-to-be.** Again, Satan is strategic. One of the strengths of a leader is the ability to avoid the traps of false loyalty. No one who genuinely loves and cares about you will require or demand that you dislike everyone that he or she dislikes. I see a lot of memes coming up on Facebook that promote false or misplaced loyalty. People tend to say things like, "I can't be friends with someone who's friends with my enemy." And while this sounds poetic, and in some cases, this may be wisdom, there are many cases where this mindset can be rendered as toxic. It's all in the context for which it is used! For example, a woman may decide that she doesn't like you simply because she's competitive, and you're not doing like everyone else in that particular setting—you're not looking to her for affirmation. You're not worshiping her or placing her on a pedestal. Instead, you are kind to her; nothing more. All the same, in that setting, you are excelling outside of her influence and without her permission. In other words, she cannot and will not get credit for your success. Let's say that this is on a job. Another woman (let's call her Evelyn) starts working at the company, and you have everything she needs to excel. Nevertheless, she notices that most of the people in that organization are esteeming the other

woman (let's call her Mandy). She wants to befriend both you and Mandy, but you don't have the power or influence that Mandy has, and after being around Mandy, she realizes that Mandy is no fan of yours, and most of the people in that setting avoid you for this very reason. Mandy has power, and she's using it for evil. Consequently, to her detriment, Evelyn follows suit and avoids you as well. She greets you, but she goes out of her way to not be seen talking with you. Believe it or not, this is extremely common because most people are followers. Most people do not want to stand out because they fear being rejected, humiliated and persecuted.

Again, I almost fell into this trap when I'd met Asia. She was way too strait-laced for my liking, but after getting to know her, I can truly say that she made a bigger impact in my life the short time (maybe two years) that we were friends than many of my former friends who'd stuck around for five plus years. Again, consider your great-grandparents. It is possible that prophetic words have been spoken over them that have yet to come to pass, and those words are like birds flying over your head, looking for a branch to land on. They've been flying over your family for years, and yes, you may be able to sense that something is close, but you haven't been able to pull it down. Think about the dove that Noah kept sending out, looking to see if the land was dry enough for him and his family to exit the ark. Genesis 8:6-12 tells the story. It reads, "And it came to pass at the end of forty days, that Noah opened the window of the ark which he had made: And he sent forth a raven, which went forth to and fro, until the waters were dried up from off the earth. Also he sent forth a dove from him, to see if the waters were abated from off the face of the ground; but the dove found no rest for the sole of her foot, and she returned unto him into the ark, for the waters were on the face of the whole earth: then he put forth his hand, and took her, and pulled her in unto him into the ark. And he stayed yet other seven days; and again he sent forth the dove out of the ark; and the dove came in to him in the evening; and, lo, in her mouth was an olive leaf pluckt off: so Noah knew that the waters were abated from off the earth. And he stayed yet other seven days; and sent forth the dove; which returned not again unto him anymore." Every blessing and every answered prayer is looking for you to get your head above the waters. Your head represents your authority and the waters represent any and everything that comes to overtake and overwhelm you. You have to bring these things under your control, after all, God has given you dominion over just about everything in the realm of the Earth, including unclean spirits.

COMING UP AND OUT OF GENERATIONAL SIN

There are two vertical directions.
- They are up and down.
- North versus South.

There are two relative directions.
- They are in and out.
- West versus East.

Look at the charts below.

Sin	Direction
←	Relative
↓	Vertical

Righteousness	Direction
→	Relative
↑	Vertical

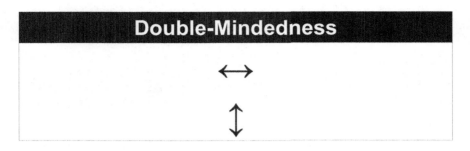

Sin	Double-mindedness	Righteousness
Egypt	Wilderness	Promised Land

The charts above are important because they serve as a visual aid to help you better understand why you or your family may have dealt with whatever it is that you've endured. If you'll notice, the chart labeled as sin has an arrow pointing left; this is what sin looks like to us, but spiritually speaking, anytime a family is headed left, they are descending. The chart labeled as righteousness displays an arrow pointing right, and of course, anytime you are heading in the right direction, you are ascending. But between both worlds, there is a wilderness. Again, this is the hallway between two seasons or mindsets. We all have to go and grow through this season, but the goal is to not get comfortable and settle down there. "A double minded man is unstable in all his ways" (James 1:8). The middle or the wilderness represents confusion; it is the space where you'll wrestle the most with God because this is the season where it literally feels like He's forsaken you. It only feels this way because you don't know Him that well. You may have been in church all of your life, served on the deacon board, been ordained and even cast out devils, but this does not mean that you truly know the heart and character of God. Religions are often established by people who know scriptures, but they don't know the Word (the person of God).

For many of us, our families have been descending for generations upon generation. We were born and raised in the pits of perversion and we've lived through events that most people wouldn't be able to survive. And then, we got saved, but that wasn't that big of a deal for most people because most or all of our family members were religious. They went to church, and some of them even served in some capacity at their local assemblies. Nevertheless, for us, it was different. We didn't just claim Jesus as our Lord and Savior, we actually started serving Him. We learned right from left, good from evil and holiness from religion. We pressed forward in an event called repentance, and we went up against the grain of our familial norms. We paid a hefty price to serve the King of kings, and we've watched others attempt to conquer this mountain as well. Howbeit, most people turned back because sin was all they knew. They hadn't counted the cost, so when they started dealing with persecution and the many degrees of warfare, they hastily turned around and resubmitted themselves back to the systems that have governed their families for generations. They returned and apologized to the narcissistic patriarchs and matriarchs that have led their families into the ditches that they call home. And for now, they are safe; they are safe from the harassment of their loved ones, the lonely seasons that most curse-breakers have to endure and the fear that plagued them whenever they tried to escape/blaze a trail for the next generation. But the problem with this is, the next generation now has to be born into this fall; they have to deal with the systems and the devils that their predecessors decided to serve. They have to face the Goliaths that their parents and grandparents decided to mate with. And by mating, I'm not talking about physical children, I'm talking about concepts, ideologies, cultures and erroneous thinking patterns that were produced and reproduced by broken and bound people. They were headed left, and they were proud of it, but when you decided to go right, what you did was called repentance. So, you went from heading left to heading right, but this was and is no easy feat. Your family had been limited to a certain region of thought, a certain income bracket and a certain end. You could almost predict how your life would turn out by simply looking at the many bound people in your family, and finding the one you could relate to the most.

Imagine this—you are living in the slums, but your house is decorated relatively well from the inside out. At the same time, you have built a lot of relationships in that slum because you can relate to the people there, after all, you grew up there. And even though your neighborhood is not the safest place to be, you feel relatively safe because you know which people to avoid, what areas to steer clear of and what hours of the day to remain inside. So, what the news calls a high crime area is home to you. But one day, you receive word that some long-lost family member of yours has passed away and he has left you everything that he owns, including a million dollar company, a savings account boasting of $50 million and a bunch of stocks and bonds valued at over one hundred million dollars. Now, you not only can afford to move out of the slums, it is NECESSARY for you t o move before word gets out that you are now a multimillionaire. Nevertheless, you love your little neighborhood and the people in it, so you stay there for a few more months, hoping that you'd be able to fix up your house and maybe even clean up the neighborhood. One day, you come home from work to discover that your house has been broken into, and the thieves have stolen just about everything you own. Thankfully, they were unable to access your bank account, so you're still a multimillionaire. You just have to start over. The police urge you to move, but you won't hear it. "I know these people, and I refuse to be another person who gets rich and runs away! Nope. I'm going to reform this neighborhood and create some youth centers for the children. These people are like family to me!" A few days later, you are robbed at gunpoint, and the robber says, "I know you're rich! Give me your pin number now!" Your saving grace happened to be a cop who was making his rounds through the neighborhood. When he spotted the robber holding you up, he brought his car to a sudden halt, and the robber took off on foot. It is in that moment that you realize that staying in that neighborhood is putting you and your children in danger, so you decide to move. You reach out to your family members and tell them about your decision, and some of them are happy, while others are so loyal to the neighborhood that's trying to kill you that they call you a sellout. You move into a safer (and more aesthetically pleasant) neighborhood, and before you can settle in good, your family starts frequenting your house. Before long, your new neighbors hate you and the police in your new city now know you by name because of the amount of calls they've received about your family members' loud music, parking violations and a few drunk uncle fights that have taken place on your front lawn and spilled over into their yards. You warn your family, but to no avail. "This is who we are! If they don't like it, they can move!" shouts one of your uncles before he takes another long sip of Patrón. Little by little, the neighbors move out, the property value plummets, and after a few years, your neighborhood now resembles the neighborhood you left behind. What was once a wealthy, quiet, well-to-do area is now a slum, and the house you paid $12 million for is now only worth $269,000. And again, your life is in danger because the people who've moved into the neighborhood are broke, but the word has gotten out that you are nowhere near broke. After being robbed at gunpoint again, you start looking at another house, but this time, you tell your family that they have to help themselves. No more handouts! "I knew this was going to happen," laughs your oldest niece. "You think you're better than us! That's what happens when folks get a little money!" But you genuinely don't think you're better than them. You've simply come to realize that you can take people out of the slums, but if they don't choose to change their minds, they will turn every neighborhood they enter into a slum.

This move is different. Your family is against you. Some of them are even trying to extort money from you. A few were being extremely nice until you made it painfully clear, once again, that you would not finance their lifestyles. "I'll pay for you to go to college so you can help yourself," you tell them, and these words weren't received well. So, you come to a wilderness season called the Big Ultimatum; this is when you're stuck between two seasons and you have to choose one over the other. If you choose your former season, everyone you know will celebrate you as you reenter the slums that God delivered you from. This doesn't change the fact that you're in danger in that neighborhood, however, because you're a multimillionaire. So, your loyalty just may cost you your life. On the other hand, you can move into a safer neighborhood, but if you do this, your family will disown you, and the ones who don't disown you will start smear campaigns. If you move forward, you stand to lose just about everything but your wealth. This is what it looks like to come against generational curses. When God blesses you with wisdom (the spiritual equivalent of wealth), this catches the attention of the people around you because, even though you're still physically there, you have moved into a new neighborhood of thinking. And to a person who's bound, your new way of seeing the world is not only offensive, it's a threat to the structure of your family. To the head narcissist of that unit, it's a threat to his or her power. Like most people, you try to help your friends and family move to a new neighborhood of thinking, but instead of them reading the books you've given them, they send them back for a refund. When they travel with you to go to a few seminars, they aren't interested in the information being shared at those seminars. They were more interested in traveling, staying at nice hotels and eating on your dollar. So, even though they are at the same hotel as you, they repeatedly urge you to go to the seminars alone because they want to go to the casinos, the malls and the clubs. It doesn't take you long to realize that you're throwing away money on them, so you start helping yourself. You buy and read the books, go to the seminars and you learn as much as you can. You get the therapy you need, you start hanging around people who live in a whole other neighborhood of reason and your perspective of the world is constantly changing. This is when you come to the Big Ultimatum. Your family is now accusing you of being high-minded, and some of them even want to physically harm you. You have to choose between two worlds; you have to choose between inferiority (your old neighborhood of thinking), mediocrity (the wilderness that you're in) and superiority (your new season). If you go back to the slums of reason, you still aren't safe, because wisdom will follow you wheresoever you go. In other words, you've had to dumb yourself down and submit to toxic beliefs. You have to choose whether or not you are willing to be like the duck who switched directions or if you'll just stay in formation; that is, deformation and conformation. This is what it looks like to cross the generational lines of bondage and enter into the wilderness (the hallway or space between two seasons). This is a time of decision and deliverance. It's a painful season, but it's necessary! Most people choose to return to their slums, even though God has given them the keys of breakthrough (revelation). This is because they don't want to be the ones to go up against the grain of toxic thinking. What about you? And going between two seasons isn't an option. People who do this often end up dealing with double-mindedness. This starts off as confusion and can graduate into a medical and spiritual condition called schizophrenia. The prefix "schizo" is a Greek word which means:

1. to rend
2. to split
3. to be divided

The suffix "phrenia," on the other hand, means the mind. So, schizophrenia means to split the mind. This is what God was referring to when He said, "A double-minded man is unstable in all his ways." And get this, most schizophrenic people are never diagnosed or treated. Most of them aren't certifiably ill, they are just religious. These people go into churches and defame their pastors, calling themselves "whistle blowers." They eventually find a church that they can change from being a religious institution to a mental institution posing as a religious institution. They sit on the front rows of these churches wearing big hats and frowns. They've learned to master their pastors by simply frowning or yawning while they're preaching. They bully just about everyone who comes into the church because they want to make it clear that they are the unofficial heads of that church. They drag their young family members to church with them, and ridicule them about everything. "Why didn't your mother comb your hair? You look like a crazy person!" or "Pull your pants up! Act like you have some home training!" These children ultimately grow up and want nothing to do with the church.

Again, there are two vertical directions. They are up and down. There are two relative directions. They are in and out. To cross generational lines and eventually set the tone for your family to get free, you have to come up and out of sin and sinful thinking. If you make a decision to move forward, please note that the warfare won't be easy, after all, you may be going up against hundreds and hundreds of years of oppression and bondage. You can't expect to defeat those devils in a day. No, Jesus overcame them for you, but now, you have to step into that freedom, and believe me when I say this—you are in for a fight, BUT it's well worth it in the end! I remember talking to a woman who'd made the hard decision to go up against the generational strongmen in her family. She'd wrestled with just about every devil underneath the sun when she was in bondage, but she was the curse-breaker in her family. She went through a lot of pain and frustration to get free, but she finally broke through the obstacles, went through one deliverance after another, and one day, she called me to tell me the good news. "Tiffany, I just watched my entire family go through deliverance!" she shouted. She was so filled with joy that she couldn't stop the tears from flowing, and I could hear her voice quivering as she relayed the news to me. She fought her way through everything from suicidal thoughts, familial opposition to every dart that Satan could find to throw at her. And when it was all over with, said and done, she'd led her once bound family to freedom. Yes, even the religious ones! Of course, everyone won't get the same results, but if one person changes directions because of you, you have done exceedingly well. You have to allow God to elevate your thinking so that He can lead you out of bondage. He will then use you to disprove the lies of Satan and lead your family out of bondage.

Note: if God separates you from some, most or all of your family members, do not try to mend those relationships outside of His timing. He wants to work on your first, and He'll do the work needed in your family before bringing you back together. If He doesn't bring you back together, it's because the family has outright rejected Him. Please be led by Him in all of your dealings. If He has to, He will custom create a family for you grafted in by His blood, and these people will give you a love that you've never experienced from before from your family. Again, it's worth it in the end!

CROSSING THE LINES

People get bound because they illegally cross boundaries; we've already established this. A boundary is nothing but a "no" or a "don't" that's been put in place by God. For example, the Bible tells us not to unequally yoke ourselves with unbelievers. This is a "don't" that God established, but when we "do" what He told us not to do, we cross a boundary and consequently end up bound. The bondage in this case is called a soul tie, and while all soul ties aren't bad, illegal connections to unbelievers will always prove to be taxing. This is because light and darkness cannot coexist. Another boundary is a common sense boundary; this means that it's not necessarily established in the scriptures that this boundary is forbidden, but we learn through education, experience and seeing the results of others what we should and should not be doing. For example, we all know not to jump into a ship, sail off into the middle of an ocean, and then, jump in the water; that is, unless we're divers, we've gotten clearance to conduct a dive, we have the proper diving gear and we have other divers out there holding us accountable. This is called a common sense boundary. Another example of a common sense boundary is—you wouldn't marry a mass murderer unless you were psychotic. And please note that not all psychotic people appear to be psychotic; some of the most demonically bound people are calm, collected, cute and careful. Their "issues" tend to manifest in their decisions, their beliefs or whenever they've been triggered. But on a normal day, they pass laws, appear on FOX News or drop another song that ends up going viral. Many of them go on to establish what we eventually accept as societal norms, thus, blurring the lines between right and wrong. Imagine it this way—there is a border separating India and Pakistan. If someone in India illegally crosses that border, he or she would be detained or shot. The same is true for a Pakistani invader. If he or she crosses the line into India, that person would be detained or shot. But I want you to imagine that this border wasn't a large fence separating the two territories, but was instead a line drawn in chalk. And while the laws in both countries dictate that someone guards those lines at all times, imagine that the governments in both countries did a lousy job in enforcing those laws. Over time, people from both sides of the border come to the chalked line when no one is around and they do their best to wipe it away. One day, the military in Pakistan see a bunch of Indian men and women picnicking on their side of the border. They confront the group who, in turn, point out that the chalked line is no longer visible. They argue that the property belongs to India, and if the men are to respond to them with violence, there will be a lot of bloodshed between both countries. The Pakistani police take the people into custody and this causes a lot of friction between both countries. Eventually, India stakes claim over the territory and the prisoners are released. A new line or border is drawn, but before long, it's blurred again. Twenty years later, Pakistan has lost a lot of ground; India has taken more than fifteen percent of its territory because of the blurred lines. This is a picture of how the enemy advances against believers and Godly systems. He goes out of his way to blur the lines between right and wrong; this way, we can unknowingly cross these lines and end up bound. All the same, he wants us to accept what God has rejected so that we'll end up slaves to ungodly systems.

Understanding Curses

One day, I decided to do research on the word "curse." God had given me so much revelation about what a curse is, and I wanted to see what others were saying. I was at the red light in my vehicle when I conducted the search, and just as the light turned green, a YouTube video popped up on my screen. The title didn't give me insight into whether the video was Christian or not, so I decided to click it anyway, hoping that I'd hear somebody talking about Jesus. I didn't. Instead, the man on the video immediately started talking about energy, light, vibrations and using a lot of New Age terminology. For about a minute, I wrestled with myself as to whether I should listen to the video or not. I'd never listened or read anything from "the other side" before, and I felt somewhat convicted at the thought of listening to the video. But on the other side of the coin, I thought to myself, "How can you help someone in that world get free if you don't know what they believe or why they believe it?" All the same, God had just given me fresh revelation about the word "curse," so I knew there was no demon that was going to attach itself to me just because I'd listened to the video. So, I decided to let it play on through. While listening to the video, I listened to the guy detail how he'd come to believe in curses. According to him, he'd experienced a lot of misfortune when he was in his twenties; it had been so bad that he started asking around, trying to find out why he kept experiencing so much hardship. He finally concluded that someone had put a curse on him. A few people told him that he wasn't cursed and that it was all in his mind, but he didn't agree. Eventually, he came across a witch who pretty much told him everything he'd felt. Like a lot of believers today, he was looking for confirmation, not information. The witch performed a cleansing ritual over him, and ever since then, he's been into New Age beliefs. He talked about the many theories that people had, most of which he didn't agree with, including the theory that his misfortune was the product of a satanic attack. He kept using his feelings as a gauge to navigate through the many theories, and he settled on the ones he'd already had in his head, which were:

1. Someone had released bad energy towards him, or pretty much put a curse on him.
2. There is no Satan or devils. He did, however, believe in angels and angelic guides.
3. He believed in the disembodied spirits of the dead trying to redeem themselves of the mistakes they'd made in their past lives.
4. He believed in reincarnation.
5. He claimed to believe in God.
6. He trusted in signs and wonders (astrology, horoscopes, etc.)

I realized after listening to him that the enemy had done to him what he tries to do with all of us; he'd put pressure on him until he became what Satan wanted him to become and not who God designed him to be. He wanted the man to become a warlock, and with enough pressure, opposition and pain, he was able to secure himself another vessel by which to work through. The guy wasn't into cursing people; he was simply the product of a lack of information and more than likely, a generational curse. After about twenty minutes, I felt like I'd listened to enough of the video, so I decided to close it.

I realized that many of the man's beliefs were not just confined to his world anymore, but have instead made their way into the church. This is because a lot of believers got saved, but they refused to undergo the sanctification process, nor were they willing to study the Word on a daily basis. Because they are used to being dependent on someone, they have chosen to sign themselves up for spiritual welfare, whereas, they rely wholly on their pastors to read the Bible to them every Sunday like a father reads a bedtime story to his children. Consequently, that's all the Bible study they get. A few show up on Tuesday or Wednesday for Bible study.

Bound People	Boundaries
Read their horoscopes.	**Deuteronomy 18:10-14:** There shall not be found among you anyone who burns his son or his daughter as an offering, anyone who practices divination or tells fortunes or interprets omens, or a

Bound People	Boundaries
	sorcerer or a charmer or a medium or a necromancer or one who inquires of the dead, for whoever does these things is an abomination to the Lord. And because of these abominations the Lord your God is driving them out before you. You shall be blameless before the Lord your God, for these nations, which you are about to dispossess, listen to fortune-tellers and to diviners. But as for you, the Lord your God has not allowed you to do this.
Practice necromancy by trying to communicate with their dead loved ones.	**Leviticus 19:31:** Regard not them that have familiar spirits, neither seek after wizards, to be defiled by them: I am the LORD your God.
Believe that their misfortune is the product of someone putting a curse on them.	**Hosea 4:6 (ESV):** My people are destroyed for lack of knowledge; because you have rejected knowledge, I reject you from being a priest to me. And since you have forgotten

Bound People	Boundaries
	the law of your God, I also will forget your children.
Looks for signs, instead of just praying and trusting God.	**Matthew 12:39:** But he answered and said unto them, An evil and adulterous generation seeketh after a sign; and there shall no sign be given to it, but the sign of the prophet Jonas.
Claim to believe in God, even though they haven't fully studied Him.	**Luke 6:46:** And why call me, Lord, Lord, and do not the things which I say?

The word "curse" is the Greek word "katara" and it is defined as:

- to go down
- condemnation
- a penalty received

Most people think that a curse is some invisible cloud of magic encircling a person and prohibiting that person from advancing. Spiritual people tend to think that a curse is a bunch of demons or bad energy surrounding a person and prohibiting that person from advancing. These misconceptions have caused a lot of believers to become religious victims who refuse to take responsibility for their own decisions. Whatever a man sows, that shall he also reap; this is scriptural, but the average Western or westernized Christian would literally beg to differ. You see, we've come to believe that most of our misfortunes are the fault of someone else, and this erroneous line of reasoning causes us to become professional victims who are both unforgiving and religious. What a toxic combo! And when people have the wrong information or beliefs about the realm of the spirit, they start trying to engage unclean spirits using carnal weapons like sage or salt. 2 Corinthians 10:4 states, "For the weapons of our warfare are not carnal, but mighty through God to the pulling down of strong holds." Please note that everything you engage with, be it natural or spiritual, has the right and the ability to respond. The only power that can hush an unclean spirit is the Word (Spirit) of God! Everything else is not only illegal, but it's useless and ineffective. Anytime you try to engage the spirit realm illegally, you are practicing witchcraft, whether you are aware of it or not.

What then is a curse? After all, when the man or woman of God stood over you and loudly proclaimed, "I break the curse off you," you likely fell to the floor and began to weep. When you got up, you felt free. So, was the curse broken? Yes, it was! But what you may not have understood was that an invisible cloud of bad energy didn't suddenly lift or fall to the ground; the chains didn't fall off your arms the way you imagined they had. Instead, what was broken is what we often refer to as oppression. Merriam-Webster defines the word "oppression" as "unjust or cruel exercise of authority or power." To get a better understanding of this term, think of the unjust treatment that the African American community has suffered for more than four-hundred years; this is called oppression. Oppression is the intentional mistreatment, subjugation, marginalization and segregation of a person or a group of people with the intent of breaking that person or that group of people; it is designed to bring a person or a group of people under the control of another person or group of people. Oppression is not an emotional response to hatred; instead, it's a calculated response to ignorance and hatred, oftentimes exercised by someone who has more power, whether that power be in natural weapons (using fear tactics, governmental seats or using verbal weapons like slander, gossip or lies) or spiritual weapons (the use of witchcraft, including astrology, palm reading, hexes, etc.) to control another human being. For example, let's say that a woman on your job looks at you and decides that she hates everything about you; she hates your voice, she hates the way that you walk, she hates your personality and she's repulsed by your line of reasoning. Because of this, she avoids you in the workplace, but she can't seem to keep her eyes off you. Whenever you enter a room that she's in, she stops what she's doing to subtly monitor your movement. The problem with this is, she's your supervisor. And to make matters worse, she doesn't think you deserve the husband that you have or the lifestyle that you have. "I'm way prettier than she is," she says to another supervisor while looking in your direction. "She thinks she's all that, but she sounds like a constipated version of Mickey Mouse! I wish she'd just shut up! Somebody needs to knock her off her high horse!" With these words, she begins to oppress you. She intentionally does not recognize your efforts or celebrate your accomplishments. She makes it a point to celebrate everyone else in your department, even though they don't perform as well as you do. Whenever she addresses you, she's condescending, dismissive and cruel. She writes you up a few times, has you demoted and does everything in her power to make you quit your job. This is called oppression; all the same, this is what a curse looks like. It isn't a cloud of dust surrounding you; it has everything to do with the region of thought that you're in and the powers (people) within that region of thought who have a measure of authority over you and access to you. Another example to consider is called a siege. This is the military equivalent of a curse. In the biblical times, a military would siege a kingdom or a city by simply surrounding it; the purpose of this tactic was to stop supplies from coming into that particular region. It was also effective in stopping the besieged city or kingdom from communicating with the outside world. Let's look at a few military tactics:

> "**Investment** is the military process of surrounding an enemy fort (or town) with armed forces to prevent entry or escape. It serves both to cut communications with the outside world, and to prevent supplies and reinforcements from being introduced.
>
> A **circumvallation** is a line of fortifications, built by the attackers around the besieged fortification facing towards an enemy fort (to protect the besiegers from

sorties by its defenders and to enhance the blockade). The resulting fortifications are known as 'lines of circumvallation'. Lines of circumvallation generally consist of earthen ramparts and entrenchments that encircle the besieged city. The line of circumvallation can be used as a base for launching assaults against the besieged city or for constructing further earthworks nearer to the city.
A **contravallation** may be constructed in cases where the besieging army is threatened by a field army allied to an enemy fort. This is a second line of fortifications outside the circumvallation, facing away from an enemy fort. The contravallation protects the besiegers from attacks by allies of the city's defenders and enhances the blockade of an enemy fort by making it more difficult to smuggle in supplies."
(Source: Wikipedia: Investment/ Military)

This is exactly what a curse looks like! But the enemy can't directly cut off your natural supplies; instead, he cuts you off from knowledge! And without knowledge, your finances will dry up or be severely limited, your relationships will dry up or you'll limit yourself to certain types of people, and your zeal will dry up. How a curse works is, it starts with an information shortage. For example, it was once considered a crime for a Black person to learn to read or write; it was also a crime for someone to teach a Black person to read or write. The goal of this was to keep Blacks reliant on Whites. When slavery ended, Blacks had to endure another level of oppression—

segregation! They were marginalized. The Black Codes enacted around 1865 were laws passed throughout the South that dictated where Blacks could work and live. The Black Codes also ensured that African Americans would provide cheap labor to their White counterparts. Blacks were limited to low-income housing projects now referred to as "ghettos." Their income was extremely limited; their education was extremely limited! Nevertheless, many Black communities began to prevail. This intimidated many racists who were determined to keep them in subjection, so they used fear tactics like public lynchings to bring Blacks back under their control. PBS.org reported the following:

> "Although the practice of lynching had existed since before slavery, it gained momentum during Reconstruction, when viable black towns sprang up across the South and African Americans began to make political and economic inroads by registering to vote, establishing businesses and running for public office. Many whites -- landowners and poor whites -- felt threatened by this rise in black prominence. Foremost on their minds was a fear of sex between the races. Some whites espoused the idea that black men were sexual predators and wanted integration in order to be with white women.
>
> Lynchings were frequently committed with the most flagrant public display. Like executions by guillotine in medieval times, lynchings were often advertised in newspapers and drew large crowds of white families. They were a kind of vigilantism where Southern white

men saw themselves as protectors of their way of life and their white women. By the early 20th century, the writer Mark Twain had a name for it: the United States of Lyncherdom."
(Source: PBS.org/American Experience/Lynching in America)

I shared this to give you insight into what a curse looks like. Spiritually speaking, what Satan does is he cuts off an individual, a family or a group of people from information. Little knowledge means low economic earning potential. Someone with low earning potential will likely live in a low-income community and be surrounded by others who have little to no education. This creates communities where crime is not only prevalent, but it becomes normal. Additionally, when there's little to no education, you will see a lot of sexual irresponsibility and immorality. One of the reasons that this happens is that people begin to develop what I call a "survivor's mindset." For example, a man with a survivor's mindset will likely commit a slew of crimes, reasoning within himself that he has to do whatever he has to do to survive. He thinks and reasons like a victim. A woman with a survivor's mindset will likely engage in promiscuity in her attempt to not only be loved, but to find someone who can provide for her. This desperation increases when she has children to feed. She then reproduces the victim's mindset in her children by blaming their fathers for her choices and her lack of resources. Children who are born into this region of thought are raised under a limited supply of information, plus, they see a culture of sexual immorality and crime. So, they perpetuate the cycles that their parents introduced them to. This is what forms a generational curse.

When you're in the wrong region of thought, chances are, it's because you were born into that pit. It's your neighborhood of thinking, your line of reasoning and your comfort zone. Consequently, you will surround yourself with people who think and reason like yourself—people who you can relate to the most. And Satan celebrates your limitations because it disallows you from getting information outside of what you already have. In other words, you keep recycling the same old information because you are afraid of being uncomfortable. So, when a woman walks into a room and she's not like you or your friends, you'll place a label on her and go out of your way to avoid building a relationship with her. You'll do this by making every encounter with her awkward or unpleasant. This is normally done through:

1. Avoiding eye contact with her.
2. Body language.
3. Being short in your responses to her.
4. Walking away or pretending to be busy when you see her heading in your direction.
5. Giving others the attention that you refuse to give to her.

Please understand that this is a cursed line of reasoning; it is a master's mindset! You also need to understand that a master doesn't just have slaves, he or she is a slave to a region of thought! What you're doing is communicating with her using non-verbal cues, and what's amazing is, we ALL know that this language is universal! In other words, she'll eventually understand what you are attempting to communicate to her. And calling her rejected is the spiritual equivalent of insulting her intelligence. In other words, you are attempting to make her feel like your inability to embrace her has everything to do with her line of reasoning when, in truth, it's your own! You see, masters feel entitled to success and power! And when they see someone who they've personally decided should remain in a second-class role, they'll do whatever they can to oppress that person! What you're doing is trying to oppress and marginalize her. Again, this is a master's mindset! This is when you have graduated from being a field slave to having slaves! This is when you have been promoted to the top of the bottom, and again, people who do this rarely escape the regions of thought they're in because they've found some measure of power and notoriety within that region. Again, please understand that this is a curse! Hurt people hurt people, but also, oppressed people oppress people! Whatever we are, we reproduce! This is why we have to get delivered; this way, we can reproduce good in the Earth!

Field Slave	House Slave	Master

The list above details the three lines of reasoning that you'll find in any given region of thought; these lines of reason, of course, are what you'll find amongst bound people.

Field Slave: This mentality is the victim's mentality. It is characterized by dependency on a system, dependency or co-dependency on people, sexual immorality, being extremely manipulative, perpetual lack, etc.

House Slave: This mentality is a follower's line of reasoning. This is usually characterized by adherence to ungodly or unproductive systems, with the sole goal being acceptance and affirmation. People reach this stage when they are accepted or embraced by a Master or someone in a position of power, and while they remain dependent or co-dependent, people within this line of reasoning serve as enforcers or enablers. Because they have been accepted by a certain group or clique, they often tell their Masters everything they know about the folks in the field. A good example of this is, let's say that Theresa works for a marketing firm where she serves as an administrative assistant. This is the bottom of her calling; it's not necessarily a low place, but it's her first step to becoming a marketing manager. Dorothy also works for the marketing firm as a marketing coordinator. Because Dorothy wants to excel to the level of a marketing specialist, she doesn't associate herself with Theresa or anyone who makes less than herself. This is a power move, of course. Howbeit, in every meeting that she goes to, she hears the marketing manager talking about Theresa's strong work ethic, some of the ideas she's submitted and her overall great attitude. Realizing that Theresa is going to be promoted, Dorothy suddenly goes out of her way to befriend her. Excited, Theresa accepts Dorothy's invitation to go out to lunch. While sitting across from Dorothy, Theresa finds herself opening up and telling her about a few of the people serving in administrative positions or in other roles. Dorothy listens and shares a few tidbits and tips about what it means to be a marketing coordinator. The two women hang out more and more, and before long, Theresa has told Dorothy just about everything she knows, from the side-conversations that go on in the break room to the rumors that are circulating around the office. What's happening is, Theresa has graduated from a field slave to a house slave.

Master: This is the top of the bottom; these are the villains, the oppressors and the power-players that crown every given region of thought. Remember, a region of thought is a season. People who reach this level have gotten some measure of influence and power within a region of thought, and instead of using that power to enter into their next seasons, they use it for evil. They are highly celebrated usurpers of authority who have been promoted into roles that allow them to acquire a measure of influence. For example, they may be the managers at your job, your Bible study teachers or Satan keeps them stuck by convincing them that they will eventually partner their way to the top. In short, they make a lot of power-moves and power-plays, hoping to hijack the top of their next seasons, rather than advance to the top through learning, dying to themselves and making the necessary sacrifices. And they almost always appear to be advancing because they do form some pretty impressive alliances, but this is just a mirage. Only God can advance us! 1 Corinthians 3:7 confirms this. It says, "So then neither is he that plants anything, neither he that waters; but God that gives the increase." Sure, people can and do get access to power, privileges and money that they are not mature enough to manage, but their positions are not to be admired because they lack the character needed to navigate those realms. This is why they become mean, competitive emotionally unstable and highly insecure. Proverbs 10:22 states, "The blessing of the LORD, it maketh rich, and he addeth no sorrow with it." The word "blessing" means "empowered to prosper." If God doesn't empower us to prosper, every other power that promotes us is illegal. Please note that another word for Master is master manipulator.

Please understand that a curse is a system. When people operate within the confines of a curse, they'll often:

1. **Find themselves surrounded by enslaved people.** When I say enslaved, I mean that these people lack information, and consequently, lack resources. So, they may find themselves locked in a region of thought that, by societal standards, is considered substandard. What this does is create familiarity and a fear of the unknown. And it is for this reason that they surround themselves with people who understand them and folks they can relate to. The word "relative" means "in proportion to." In layman's terms, they surround themselves with other people who are in bondage. Additionally, if and when they try

to befriend people who are outside of their regions of thought, they are often rejected because they are viewed as liabilities.

2. **Fear success.** This is often the product of what they've been told. For example, growing up, I often heard many of my family members referring to other family members who'd gone to college, escaped poverty and gone out of their way to better themselves as high-minded. Because of this, many of us (children) reasoned within ourselves that success automatically equated to being prideful, so we found ourselves saying things like, "If I ever made it, I wouldn't act like that" or "If I ever made it, I wouldn't change. I'm gonna keep it real!" We said this, not realizing that we were being taught to see change as an enemy when, in truth, change is necessary for true success. Consequently, any time we were required to do anything that would facilitate a change to our minds, we would quit, hoping that we'd get what we needed another way.

3. **Ensnare themselves.** They do this by pledging a bunch of agreements with people, from family members to friends to romantic interests to loan agencies. People who are slaves to a system wear bondage like bracelets. You can see this manifesting in a lot of low income areas, for example, a woman who lives in poverty will get her income tax, and instead of putting the money up for a rainy day, she'll buy a car that she can't afford and go into bondage

trying to pay those car notes and insurance.

4. **Develop a survivor's mindset.** This encourages the person to become manipulative. In truth, manipulation expresses itself through every vein in their bodies. What this looks like is, they'll try to get you to pay for their food if you go out to eat, they're always flattering you and they're always strategically partnering up with people who have some measure of power. They rarely, if ever, take responsibility for themselves, often playing the damsels in distress, especially when they're around people they perceive to be in a better position than themselves.

5. **Sabotage themselves.** One of the laws that we learn as we advance through each region of thought is—when you come across someone who outranks you, listen more than you speak! But someone with a slave mentality will over-talk the folks that they should be listening to; they will also try to gain favor by talking nonstop about themselves, attempting to flatter others or casting themselves as victims. This only serves to sabotage them because people who have the information that they need to escape their seasons then begin to avoid them because they aren't listeners. Instead, they are trying to pour when they should be receiving an impartation. This is to say that if you are rejected by a person, this doesn't necessarily mean that the person is bad, it could be because you keep trying to teach the teacher.

6. **Sabotage others.** We call this the "crabs in the

bucket" mentality. In the slums of thinking, there is a lot of entitlement, and anytime you see entitlement, you'll see jealousy. Jealousy is often provoked by a series of ungodly beliefs, with the most prominent being the belief that you are more qualified or deserving of something, whether its a position or a person, than someone else. These thoughts are then followed up by a bunch of negative thoughts about the person in question. You'll keep thinking like this until you develop the belief that you have the right to say what's on your mind regarding the person. What you're doing is operating in low-level sabotage, and when that's unsuccessful, you'll likely escalate your behaviors until you're operating in full-blown witchcraft. In other words, if you allowed yourself to fall into this trap, you'd become part of Satan's network; these are the tools and people that he uses to stop another human being from advancing.

Within the walls of a curse, you'll find yourself needing information and help that's not readily available to you. What makes this difficult is the fact that you can sense that the information or whatever it is that you need is out there, and sometimes, it feels like it's within reach, but you don't know how to access or grasp it. So, let's say that you need twenty bucks to feed your children, but you have a low-paying job and you won't be getting paid for another four days. None of your friends or family members have two nickels to rub together, but you know that if you looked long and hard enough, you could find what you need somewhere. It's out there, but because you have limited connections, you can't seem to find it. Consequently, you go and put yourself deeper into debt by getting a loan. Some people even resort to selling drugs or engaging in prostitution to make ends meet. And they may reason within themselves that what they're doing is temporary; that is, until they get, for example, an income tax check or a raise on their jobs. Nevertheless, years later, they find themselves still doing the same thing to make ends meet because it's what they've mastered or, better yet, been mastered by. If this isn't difficult enough, every chance to escape that region of thought is met by resistance from the people around you, resistance from the people who are crowing that region of thought and a lack of information and the people who've mastered that region of thought. This is why the Bible tells us that we have to take the Kingdom of Heaven by force! What this means is you have to pull out your potential and walk past, confront and overcome every force that dares to serve as opposition to your ascension. One of the lessons I learned is that the greatest amount of pressure and warfare does not come from the crabs in the bucket; they pinch you, it hurts and you literally get over it. The real pressure comes from the top; it comes from the people you expect to pull you up, but instead, they will try to place a lid (label) on you to keep you down. When I first started experiencing this back in around 2010, I found myself crying before the Lord and asking why. I didn't have a church home and I didn't have anyone in my life that could help me to put language to what I was experiencing. I'd started manifesting my potential, and jealousy came after me head-on! So I prayed about it. God answered me with a scripture. Matthew 20:1-16 (ESV) gives us insight into the minds and hearts of broken people. It reads, "For the kingdom of heaven is like a master of a house who went out early in the morning to hire laborers for his vineyard. After agreeing with the laborers for a denarius a day, he sent them into his vineyard. And going out about the third hour he saw others standing idle in the marketplace, and to them he said, 'You go into the vineyard too, and whatever is right I will give you.' So they went. Going out again about the sixth hour and the ninth hour, he did the same. And about the eleventh hour he went out and found others standing. And he said to them, 'Why do you stand here idle all day?' They said to him, 'Because no one has hired us.' He said to them, 'You go into the vineyard too.' And when evening came, the owner of the vineyard said to his foreman, 'Call the laborers and pay them their wages, beginning with the last, up to the first.' And when those hired about the eleventh hour came, each of them received a denarius. Now when those hired first came, they thought they would receive more, but each of them also received a denarius. And on receiving it they grumbled at the master of the house, saying, 'These last worked only one hour, and you have made them equal to us who have borne the burden of the day and the scorching heat.' But he replied to one of them, 'Friend, I am doing you no wrong. Did you not agree with me for a denarius? Take what belongs to you and go. I choose to give to this last worker as I give to you. Am I not allowed to do what I choose with what belongs to me? Or do you begrudge my generosity?' So the last will be first, and the first last." Again, this is a cursed mindset! This doesn't mean that the person is accursed; they are oftentimes saved, however, the systems of thinking that they've surrendered themselves to are accursed. This is what keeps them from prospering or actualizing their full potential. You see, a curse isn't a black cloud of smoke surrounding a person, it's a mindset!

I'm sure some people will ask, "Well, if that's the case, what does a witch do? If someone hires a witch to put a curse on somebody, how does that work?" It's simple! Satan has agents everywhere! Most of them don't realize they are agents of Satan. He also has hired workers; these are people who are a part of another system (believers) who he can readily use if the price is right. And by price, I'm not just talking about money! Satan looks for cravings; these are desires that haven't been quenched, and if he finds them, he'll promise to fulfill those desires if only the people who have them agree to do to a few jobs for him. And in this, I'm trying to careful with my language because I don't want you to see this as an actual audible conversation that these people hear. No, the majority of them don't realize they are being used by the enemy. Instead, they just have something on their minds that they want, and they haven't given that desire to God. When Satan goes about seeking who he can devour, he's looking for people who are outside the will of God. Whenever he finds believers, he finds out whatever it is that they want and then he shows them illegal ways to acquire it. For example, if a believing woman desires to be married and she hasn't given that desire to God, chances are, Satan knows her "type." So, Satan won't just tempt her, he'll tempt a few men who he believes to be perfect fits for her—men who he can use to hurt her and conform her into the woman he wants her to be. Of course, these men will be double-minded and unstable, nevertheless, Satan will allow her to see their potential. This is what I call a demonic strip tease. We all have potential. Even your local crack or heroin addict has potential, but when Satan wants to ensnare a woman, he makes a man's potential appear to be within her reach. So, in conversation, the man may open up to her and tell her things that he hasn't told anyone else; this makes her feel comfortable and it gives her a level of responsibility in his life. She now has to guard what he's shared with her. Slowly, but surely, the two will create a bond (soul tie), and before long, she will give Satan the sin offering he needs to advance. In this, Satan will attack her credibility and attempt to lock her into a region of thought. This is effective if the agent he used is locked in and committed to that region of thought. So, she sacrifices her future on the altar of idolatry, planning within her head and her heart to eventually give God back His place in her life; that is, after she's gotten what she wants first, which is—marriage. This is a trap inside of a curse! But believe it or not, it's one of Satan's most effective weapons! What she's doing is attempting to hijack her next season, and this is illegal! The man in question may be a believer, but because he's not fully submitted to God, he is on Satan's payroll. And again, he's not sitting in some dark room having a conversation with the devil! He's not intentionally trying to stop her from advancing; he's dealing with temptation just like she is, and get this—she may also be an enemy against his potential! Both of them will serve to lock one another into a region of thought or a season of mediocrity! So, what does a witch do? It's simple. A witch or a warlock communicates with demonic spirits! Guess what the bound guy who came after the bound woman had? They both had a need for deliverance! They had voids that hadn't been filled, and the enemy lives in voids; he lives in darkness! They had appetites that overwhelmed them! In short, a witch's job is to communicate with the demonic realm. The goal is to stop the advancement of b God's people from one season to the next. Let's look at another example! If a pastor was traveling to Cambodia for a missions' trip, and word got out about his plans, a witch in Cambodia may find out the news and become agitated. Of course, those familiar spirits she's housing are terrified, especially if the pastor is known to cast out demons. So, she may pray to her deity and offer sacrifices to her deity to stop the arrival of that pastor. All of a sudden, a few people in America surrounding the pastor may start discouraging him. If this doesn't work, he may find himself having a hard time getting his passport approved. In other words, there's a bound person in the passport office who may be reviewing his application. Again, the person isn't hearing an audible voice; in most cases, the person is just triggered by a series of emotions, thoughts and inconveniences. After some praying and pushing, the passport is finally approved, but the fight isn't over. The pastor suddenly receives a call from his employer stating that the company is laying some people off, and he may be on the chopping block. This is designed to provoke fear in his heart and get him to cancel his trip. But let's say that this doesn't work. All of a sudden, his fiance starts getting cold feet and thinking about calling off their wedding. Do you see all of the lines of communication the enemy has? The witch simply sent out a notice of sorts into the demonic realm, and Satan used every demon that had direct or indirect access to that guy through personal relationships and non-personal relationships to oppress him on every side. But let's say that he still plans his trip, despite the threats of losing his job and his future bride. Chances are, he'll get some more warfare at the airport, both in the United States and then in Cambodia. Once he gets through the airport, he still has the hotel and every other venue to look forward to! Satan uses a network of people to carry out his agenda. Again, a curse is not a black cloud of supernatural smoke with sparkles in it. It's the use of bound people to oppress people! This is what we call a demonic system.

Mark 4:35-39: And the same day, when the even was come, he saith unto them, Let us pass over unto the other side. And when they had sent away the multitude, they took him even as he was in the ship. And there were also with him other little ships. And there arose a great storm of wind, and the waves beat into the ship, so that it was now full. And he was in the hinder part of the ship, asleep on a pillow: and they awake him, and say unto him, Master, carest thou not that we perish? And he arose, and rebuked the wind, and said unto the sea, Peace, be still. And the wind ceased, and there was a great calm.

In this scripture, we see another level of warfare. The winds were pressing up against the ship that Jesus was on, and the waters began to fill the vessel. The men were on their way to Gadarenes, a demon-infested city on the eastern shore of Galilee. Where did those winds come from? The Greek word for breath is the same word for "wind" and "spirit." You'll notice that the majority of countries that are largely hit by hurricane winds and tornadoes every year are countries that are filled with witches. What they are releasing is what the bible calls "contrary winds." This is to say that the warfare Jesus and His crew faced wasn't a big demon in the sky pushing them with its breath; it was a collection of voices from people who were bound. Look at what happened once Jesus arrived in Gadarenes. Mark 5:1-13 tells us a familiar store. It reads, "And they came over unto the other side of the sea, into the country of the Gadarenes. And when he was come out of the ship, immediately there met him out of the tombs a man with an unclean spirit, who had his dwelling among the tombs; and no man could bind him, no, not with chains: Because that he had been often bound with fetters and chains, and the chains had been plucked asunder by him, and the fetters broken in pieces: neither could any man tame him. And always, night and day, he was in the mountains, and in the tombs, crying, and cutting himself with stones. But when he saw Jesus afar off, he ran and worshiped him, and cried with a loud voice, and said, What have I to do with thee, Jesus, thou Son of the most high God? I adjure thee by God, that thou torment me not. For he said unto him, Come out of the man, thou unclean spirit. And he asked him, What is thy name? And he answered, saying, My name is Legion: for we are many. And he besought him much that he would not send them away out of the country. Now there was there nigh unto the mountains a great herd of swine feeding. And all the devils besought him, saying, Send us into the swine, that we may enter into them. And forthwith Jesus gave them leave. And the unclean spirits went out, and entered into the swine: and the herd ran violently down a steep place into the sea, (they were about two thousand;) and were choked in the sea." This was the reason that the winds met the men at sea! When you're between two seasons or regions of thought, you will oftentimes endure some of your greatest warfare. Again, this space or stretch of time is the hallway between two seasons. It is designed to get you to stop advancing and to return to the region of thought you've come from.

Next, let's deal with the misnomer that a Christian can't operate under a curse. Christians can't be accursed, but they can operate under a curse. Witches know this; warlocks know this, and other ungodly mediums know this. It's the believer who tends to be ignorant of this fact. This is why God said, "My people perish for lack of knowledge." There are some systems that are ungodly; the Bible refers to them as the "systems of this world." Ungodly systems (mindsets) are cursed, and anyone who embraces those mindsets receives the fruits thereof. The word "accursed" means to be without God or without His blessing. A system that is not backed or approved by God will be riddled with demons. Today, you'll come across many believers who think and reason as the world does, and you'll notice that they tend to live like the world and receive the same plagues that the world receives. This is because they got saved, but they refused to endure the sanctification process. Instead, they pointed out a few double-minded believers who had greater rank than themselves, and they pointed out a few people who've fallen while ascending, and then, they used that information to justify their refusals to leave the regions of thought that they're in. I hear a lot of believing women say that they don't want the church guy because he's a hypocrite, but in truth, they've never allowed God to acclimate their appetite to holiness, so they are allergic to men who don't have rap sheets. This is a region of thought or season that they've committed themselves to, and unfortunately, many of them spend their lives in mediocrity and chaos because they keep looking for blessings in landfills. So while they may not be cursed, they are operating under a system that is cursed. If they were to undergo the sanctification process and allow God to give them a new heart and a new mind, they'd step into their true identities, their authority and their rightful places. But the journey between that place and where they are is pretty rocky, and they have to develop enough knowledge and determination to will themselves out of that system.

And lastly, curses can be self-inflicted. Proverbs 6:1-5 reads, "My son, if thou be surety for thy friend, if thou hast stricken thy hand with a stranger, thou art snared with the words of thy mouth, thou art taken with the words of thy mouth. Do this now, my son, and deliver thyself, when thou art come into the hand of thy friend; go, humble thyself, and make sure thy friend. Give not sleep to thine eyes, nor slumber to thine eyelids. Deliver thyself as a roe from the hand of the hunter, and as a bird from the hand of the fowler." The word "surety" means:

- a formal engagement (such as a pledge) given for the fulfillment of an undertaking: guarantee
- a basis of confidence or security
- one who has become legally liable for the debt, default, or failure in duty of another

(Source: Merriam-Webster)

Another word for "surety" is "insurance." Someone who makes themselves liable for the deeds of another person is called a "bondsman" or "bondswoman." A bondsman fills out the bonding paperwork for an individual, collects the fine owed by that individual and tracks down the individual if he or she does not appear in court. A bondsman assumes the responsibility of a bond in hopes that the accused person will pay him back (with interest). Here's a thought—many of the people that we meet when we're in the wrong region of thought are bound. All too often, what we do is befriend, date, partner up with and marry these people. We do this because, like bail bondsmen, we believe that they'll eventually repay us for our good deeds (with interest). When the enemy wants to keep you in a region of thought, he will throw bound people at you! Remember, a curse is similar to a military siege; the goal is to surround you with the wrong people so that new information cannot come in and you either become too comfortable or too scared to get out of the bondage that you once committed yourself to. In this, your soul tie will serve as a set of ropes and chains. Think about this—a man can get out of a set of handcuffs if he's willing to bleed. If he's willing to endure the pain associated with breaking the bones in his hands, he can get out of bondage, but the fear of pain coupled with the fear of the authority who's binding him is enough to keep him in compliance. The same is true for an ungodly soul tie. A bound person can get free, but it's going to be painful, scary and humiliating. That person would have to be willing to break his or her own heart by tugging on that soul tie until it snaps. Most people aren't willing to endure this level of pain, and Satan knows this. So, he fashions soul ties as handcuffs and looks for anyone who's wanting to hijack their next season. This is an example of self-inflicted bondage. Another example is through confessions. Oftentimes, when we're emotional, we make declarations that eventually come back to haunt us. Just like a witch releases winds of warfare against people by chanting and praying to demonic spirits, we can release winds of warfare against ourselves by opening our mouths and saying things that we should not say. Another great example of this is when a woman who's been hurt opens her mouth and says, "All men are cheaters!" This isn't a truth, but what she's doing is shaping her world with her words. Consequently, every man she meets and links herself up to romantically will be damaged in the Eros (romantic) state and consequently, he will cheat on her. What she's done is summoned those men through the use of her tongue.

Again, a curse is not magic; it's just a system of failure that's secured and carried out by bound people. So, the next time somebody says that they've put a curse on you, do what Jesus did to the winds—rebuke their words! Use the Word of God against their words! Whenever you experience the winds of opposition coming against you, remember this— opposition is the opposing of your position! The way to counter it is by cutting off its head (authority) with the Word of God.

UNDERSTANDING THE STORMS OF LIFE

A weather pattern is the behavior of the weather in any particular region during a specific season. Think about the state of Florida. It's known for its hurricanes, California is known for its earthquakes, Mississippi is known for its flooding and tornadoes, Arizona is known for its droughts, Colorado is known for its freezing temperatures, and both Texas and California are known to have a lot of wildfires during the summer months because of their dry vegetation and warm temperatures. The South tends to get a lot of hurricanes and tornadoes during the Spring, whereas, the North tends to get a lot of snow storms during the Winter months. These are what we call weather patterns, and again, you'll notice that they are common in specific regions. The same is true for the warfare that we call the storms of life.

Regions of Thought		
	North	
East		West
	South	

- **North:** Mature Believer
- **South:** Immature Believer, Carnal Believer, Unsaved People

- **East and West:** Wandering (Deviating) Believer

You'll notice that some people rarely deal with the storms that many of us face. It's not because they are exempt from warfare, it is oftentimes because they live in a specific region of thought (season). In every region of thought, there is a specific type of warfare that's common to that particular season. For example, if you are a woman trying to date while in one of the southern regions of thought, chances are, you've dealt with your fair share of men who've wooed you out of your clothes and then, walked away. The south represents low thinking. Of course, I'm not talking about the Southern states; I'm using directional terminology to describe what's good versus what's not-so-good. When you come across a guy in the southside of reasoning, chances are, he's a slave. The question is, which unclean spirit is he a slave to? Is it Mammon, the demonic deity that promotes the love of money? Is it rejection? Did his father leave him when he was young, only for his mother to expose him to a series of men who all entered his life, and then, left without as much as a goodbye? Consequently, he's perpetuating the same cycle, because subconsciously, he thinks this is what it means to be a man. Is it lust and perversion? Was he raped, molested or subjected to an environment where lust was commonplace or even celebrated? Either way, he needs healing, deliverance and new information, and you're not the one who's been "sent" to give it to him, especially if you're romantically interested in him or vice versa. I tell people all the time that sex and evangelism don't mix. You've simply come across a person and/or a spirit that you're interested in or familiar with, plus, you can see the potential behind that man's issues. Every human being has potential, but when the enemy tries to woo you into a relationship that God warned you not to enter, he will oftentimes employ a tactic that I call a demonic strip tease. In this, the enemy allows you to see the potential of a person and the good side of that person. This is when a man will look you in the eyes and tell you all the bad things that happened to him (drunk, belligerent, negligent mother; cheating ex; absent or abusive father, etc.). A few sentences later, the enemy will begin to highlight that guy's potential. You'll get a sneak peak into what you could potentially have if you are to enter into an agreement (soul tie) with the guy. This is a demonic strip tease. Satan simply allowed you to see a snapshot of who that man was created by God to be so that you could spend the next few years trying to rescue him from himself. Consequently, the people who fall into this trap marry or have babies with the weapons that were formed against them, and they spend years and tears trying to pull out the potential in their significant or insignificant others. And every time they reason within themselves that they are going to leave those relationships and reset their lives, the enemy gives them another strip show. The guy comes home and apologizes, highlighting his fears and his shortcomings, and then, follows it up with, "I know you're going to leave me. Everybody I love leaves me, but it's cool." You'll find a lot of guys and girls like this on the southside of reason. As a matter of fact, you'll find that idolatry is commonplace on this level. Please note that there are many manifestations of idolatry, which include, but are not limited to:

1. **Relational (Romantic) Idolatry:** In this, you'll see women who don't know how to be alone; they find their value in relationships, so they go from one man to the other, hoping that some guy will eventually see their worth (or potential), marry them and make their lives better. Women on this side of reason tend to idolize marriage and men. Men on this level tend to idolize or glorify sex and/or money.

2. **Addiction to Oxytocin:** Called the "love hormone," oxytocin partners with dopamine to create a surge of emotions in an event that we refer to as "falling in love" or "being in love." Some people are literally addicted to this high! They are addicted to the proverbial "cloud nine" effect! Women tend to idolize marriage, but men tend to idolize this feeling! Some men enter into relationships and begin to rush those relationships (in psychology, they call it "love bombing") by saying things like, "I know we haven't talked long enough for me to say this, but I think I'm in love with you" or "I don't know what's happening to me because I can't stop thinking about you!" Sure, some guys are lying when they say this, but most are being truthful! They are experiencing high-level "hormonal activity," and in that moment, they are just going with the flow. What this does is encourages a woman who has idolized marriage or men to lower her guards all the more and allow herself to freely flow

into the same experience. She feels free to let dopamine dope her into giving up the password to her heart, taking off her clothes and fully surrendering herself to the man she's entertaining. But like any drug, oxytocin eventually wears off! Sometimes, this happens three years and two kids later. In other words, one or both parties will eventually sober up and the relationship ultimately ends when one sober person wants out of it or two sober people realize that they don't really like each other. The guy will then go out and "love bomb" someone else and genuinely experience the highs and lows of oxytocin all over again. Five children and two restraining orders later, you'll find him at it again with a new woman and another court date.

3. **Relational (Familial) Idolatry:** This typically happens in families where the matriarch or patriarch of the family is bound by what the world calls "narcissism" or what the church calls the Jezebel spirit. In these types of environments, children are taught to put "blood over water," meaning to put family before anything and anyone else. And this is sometimes so deeply engraved within the fabric of a family that most of the women either do not get married or cannot stay married because of their beliefs. The guys are the same, but many of them will normally find women who will grow to accept their unnatural affections toward their mothers or other family members. If they say something about this behavior or question it, they are

often accused of trying to come between the guy and his family, and this is a pretty harsh accusation to weather, so many of the women just accept it until they simply can't take it anymore or until they are discarded by the men. Nevertheless, we all should love and honor our families; that's a given, however, in the Kingdom of God, there is order. Anything that is outside of God's will is labeled as "disorderly conduct," and this is the very fabric of a dysfunctional family.

4. **Relational (Platonic) Idolatry:** You'll see both men and women who idolize their friends, oftentimes because they've been through a lot with the opposite sex, and they've come to believe that their friends will be there for them when no one else can or will. Consequently, they put their friends before their spouses, their children, their parents and of course, God.

5. **The Love of Money:** On the southside of reason, you will come across a lot of men blasting music that promotes sexual immorality, violence and the love of money! You will come across men and women who are willing to beg, cheat and steal to get the lifestyles they are so desperately in love with. It's great to want to provide for yourself and your family, but when you are willing to do anything to make this happen, chances are, you are bound by Mammon and living in the southside of reason.

6. **The Love of Power:** This idolatrous thinking pattern

is normally paired up with the love of money (Mammon). It's usually rooted in the spirits of witchcraft and control, and instigated by the spirit or strongman of rejection. People who lack integrity typically want power so that they can control and manipulate others.

7. **Dependency (Substance):** On the southside of reason, you will come across people who ware either addicted to alcohol or drugs or people who abuse some other substance. This is because when people lack knowledge, feel oppressed and deal with a lot of guilt and shame, they typically try to find ways to escape their pain. Alcohol and drugs allow them to feel as if they have escaped, but in truth, they only serve to further complicate things.

8. **Dependency (Lifestyle):** We call these "comfort zones," and many people who are on the southside of logic tend to make idols out of them. This is largely due to the fear of the unknown, coupled with the lies and misconceptions they've been taught by people who claim to know what it's like on the "other side" of reason.

All of these lines of reason are weather patterns or mindsets, and if pair your heart with someone who has a contrary way of thinking, a storm is inevitable. Storms are usually the product of two contrary regions of thought attempting to merge together. "Be ye not unequally yoked together with unbelievers: for what fellowship hath righteousness with unrighteousness? And what communion hath light with darkness?" (2 Corinthians 6:14). To get a better understanding of storms, check out the article below.

"A weather front is a transition zone between two different air masses at the Earth's surface. Each air mass has unique temperature and humidity characteristics. Often there is turbulence at a front, which is the borderline where two different air masses come together. The turbulence can cause clouds and storms. Instead of causing clouds and storms, some fronts just cause a change in temperature. However, some storm fronts start Earth's largest storms. Tropical waves are fronts that develop in the tropical Atlantic Ocean off the coast of Africa. These fronts can develop into tropical storms or hurricanes if conditions allow."

(Source: UCAR Center for Science Education/Weather Fronts)

It's amazing how God uses the natural to explain spiritual things! Jesus spoke to the Church of Laodicea in Revelation 3:16 and said, "I know thy works, that thou art neither cold nor hot: I would thou wert cold or hot. So then because thou art lukewarm, and neither cold nor hot, I will spue thee out of my mouth." What Christ is dealing with here is mixture! That church was caught between two paralleling worlds! On one hand, they claimed to be Christians who loved the Lord, but on the other hand, they trusted in their own wealth. This is evidenced in Revelation 3:17-18, where Jesus goes on to say, "Because thou sayest, I am rich, and increased with goods, and have need of nothing; and knowest not that thou art wretched, and miserable, and poor, and blind, and naked: I counsel thee to buy of me gold tried in the fire, that thou mayest be rich; and white raiment, that thou mayest be clothed, and that the shame of thy nakedness do not appear; and anoint thine eyes with eyesalve, that thou mayest see." According to the Lord, they were neither hot nor cold; in other words, they were neutral! They were self-centered, egotistical, double-minded and religious! But remember, when hot air mixes with cold air, it produces a front! Amazingly enough, the word "front" in slang means to put on a false persona; it means to be pretentious.

Think about some of the people you've come in contact with who almost always seem to have some type of issue arising in their lives. Most of their problems stem from mixture. In other words, they have the wrong people in their lives or they have the right people in the wrong areas of their lives. There are levels of intimacy, and not everyone can be close to your heart; some people make great acquaintances, but horrible friends. Some people make great friends, but horrible spouses. But if you allow them into an area or into a role that they are not fit for, again, a storm is inevitable. Amazon wouldn't hire a high school dropout with questionable character, and give that person a seat as one of their directors! No, most companies screen their employees; they look for diplomas, degrees and experience! They also conduct background checks! Now, Amazon could potentially hire a high school dropout to serve in another role like package delivery, but they won't give that person a role that could potentially sink the company. Nevertheless, most believers date, court and marry folks who they have not screened! The short of it is, storms are almost always the products of wrongful relationships or right relationships done the wrong way. Most of what we call depression is nothing but a cocktail of dreams, regrets and issues that have arisen with the people around us. I have counseled people, for example, who were angry, suicidal and on the brink of insanity simply because they refused to separate themselves from their toxic parents or family members. Telling someone that they need to cut ties with a family member is never an easy conversation, nevertheless, if the options available in that person's mind are to either kill themselves, kill their family members or walk away and heal, the better option is obvious—they need to walk away. And in most cases, I advise them to simply put distance between themselves and their parents or their loved ones. What this means is, they may need to go from talking to them everyday to speaking with them once or twice a month; they may have to stay away from their parents' or loved ones' homes and only invite them out into a neutral space like a restaurant, but end all meetings when and if the conversation starts taking a dark turn. Sadly enough, most people aren't willing to listen to this. They have romanticized the idea of having the Brady Bunch experience with a family who has the mental and moral capacity of the Adam's Family, so they spend their lives:

1. Imagining how good their families would be if they

were to get their acts together.

2. Seeing other healthy families and then getting angry and jealous because their families are nothing like those families.

3. Trying to change their family members by talking to them, arguing with them, showing them videos of healthy, non-toxic families, etc.

4. Getting disappointed time and time again whenever their efforts to change their family are met with resistance and opposition.

5. Fantasizing about killing themselves or their family members as punishment for not becoming who they had the potential to become.

This is a cycle that they repeat month after month and year after year! Consequently, many of them leave this Earth prematurely because they would not and could not find peace. It's not because peace didn't exist or because it wasn't within their reach, after all, peace is available for everyone! The problem with them is, they didn't want to make the sacrifices needed to find, acquire and sustain an atmosphere for peace! Peace is the product of right alignment! And I'm not talking about any New Age foolishness, I'm talking about being aligned with the right people in the right way! It's okay to have relationships, for example, with toxic family members, but you shouldn't attempt to have intimate relationships with them, for example, I have relatives who have absolutely no respect for God or order. If I were to open my house or heart to them, they'd bring chaos into my life. This is because they have a contrary way of thinking; they are not only affiliated with the wrong people, but they themselves are extremely toxic. So, I created and enforced boundaries with them. Do they like those boundaries? Not at all! They interpret boundaries as a sign that they are being rejected. And because I've established and consistently enforced my boundaries, I am labeled as the family member who "thinks she's better than everybody" and the person who "needs to be knocked off her high horse." These terms are common in the southside of reason. I once lived in that region of thought and I once embraced the ideologies of that world; that is, until I decided that I wanted to do better and be better. I watched my mother try to man her way through storms that were created simply because she refused to close doors that needed to be closed. Like most people, she wanted so passionately to have a strong family unit, but the truth of the matter is, there are some people you will never have a strong connection with. This is because they don't want anything to do with God, and no amount of evangelism is going to change their minds. They love chaos and they are in love with dysfunction! This is why Jesus said, "Who are my mother and my brothers? Those who do the will of God; they are my mother and my brothers!" Nevertheless, many people give up the ghost prematurely because they feared the hallway between two seasons. Again, this is the Red Sea and the wilderness that separates one season from the other. In the wilderness, many of the people who cannot walk into your next season with you will fall away. God uses the wilderness to wash away the residue from your former season! Howbeit, many people refuse to get the information they need to walk out of the seasons they're in because they have the same line of reasoning that the people had who attempted to build the Tower of Babel. They want the benefits of a better world or a better life, but not the responsibilities that precede it!

So, in short, a storm is the response of two worlds attempting to merge. All the same, it's important to note that all mergers that create storms aren't bad. For example, if you are in the wrong region of thought, God will oftentimes send leaders and mentors to offend the way that you think. Their line of reasoning will meet your line of reasoning, and they will clash! Some of the most intense storms you'll ever find yourself in are the ones where God is shifting the way that you think through correction and connection! In that moment, you'll have a choice. You can submit to the correction and pray your way through all of the negative emotions and offenses that surface or you can run away. People who choose to find leaders and mentors who don't offend their way of thinking are people who ultimately end up religious and stuck!

Understanding Demonic Residue

Imagine that you are a woman walking through the mall when all of a sudden, a group of men start cat-calling you. This is something that you're accustomed to, so you don't put too much thought into it. But after you've walked past a few stores and found your way into the dining area, you see what appears to be the most handsome man you've ever seen. He's sitting alone, reading a Bible. You subtly scan his right hand to see if he has a wedding ring on his finger. All clear! So, you sit a few tables away from him, facing in his direction, hoping that he'll look up and see your pretty face. He does. He notices your body language and the fact that you don't seem to be as heavily engaged with your phone as you're pretending to be. So, he looks away trying to figure out the best approach to take. Realizing that he's unsure about how to approach you, you make the first move. "Excuse me. Do you know what time it is? My phone's screen is cracked, so I can't see the time feature." He giggles inwardly as he thinks to himself, "You could have searched Google for that, but okay." Knowing that you're as interested in him as he is in you, he responds, "It's 3:15. Why? Does your man have you on a curfew?" Five minutes later after you two have finished your verbal mating ritual, he makes his way over to your table and the two of you start talking all the more. You exchange numbers, and a year later, the two of you are still a couple. Everywhere the two of you have gone together, people have said, "You are so cute together!" You blush, hoping that the compliment makes your beau feel as blessed to be with you as you feel to be with him. He's a great guy, but you've discovered some things about him that aren't so integral, even though he frequents church and is an ordained minister at the church that he attends. Before long, you have a term to tag him with that perfectly fits his personality—narcissist. Your boyfriend is narcissistic. But he's saved, so you reason within yourself that he's the way that he is because of what he's been through. His mother abused and mishandled him. His father abandoned him when he was three-years old. His grandmother raised him for the majority of his life, but she was a narcissistic alcoholic who hated men, so she verbally castrated him every chance she got. Knowing what's wrong with him makes him appear to be "fixable." Nevertheless, after a pregnancy scare, he does the unthinkable. He cheats on you with one of his ex-girlfriends, and then, abruptly exits your life. This is a pattern you've seen one too many times before! Once again, you find yourself on your ex's Facebook page, scrolling through his pictures, trying to look for clues. Your eyeliner has mixed with your tears, and your heart feels like it's about to explode into a million pieces. A few minutes later, someone tags you in a video about demonic residue and patterns. After listening to the video, you realize that there is a pattern present in your life. You tend to attract a certain type of man; you attract men who passionately pursue you for about a year before cheating on you and then discarding you whenever you discover their indiscretions.

This is the same pattern you saw in your mother's relationships and in your sisters' relationships. You realize in that moment that you have some demonic residue attached to you.

Like most believers, when you hear the term "demonic residue," you're likely envisioning some invisible substance or an invisible scent that attracts people to you. And because you think this way, chances are, you'll find yourself at the altar come next Sunday, looking for someone to "wash away" the residue. As Christians, we tend to over-spiritualize the issues that we find ourselves wrestling with; this is oftentimes because we lack understanding, and in some cases, we tend to do this because we genuinely don't want the responsibility of changing our behavior. So, you point at the devil, blame him for your misfortune, stand at the altar, and bawl away as the minister prays over you. You fall to the floor, imagining that when you get up, your situation will have changed for the better. All of your ungodly soul ties will be broken, the demonic residue will be power-washed away and life will become much easier from there. Three Sundays later, you find yourself back at the altar, thinking that the person who laid hands on you the first time clearly wasn't powerful enough to deal with your issues. Maybe, she had some unchecked sin in her life or maybe, what you're dealing with is much bigger than her. You mentally pick out the minister that you want to pray for you, and then, you make your way towards the section where you see that minister standing. You lift your head, close your eyes, cry, wait and pray. And that's when you feel a hand on your shoulders. You open your eyes only to see that same girl who prayed for you three Sundays ago standing in front of you. Disappointed, you close your eyes again and try to figure out your next move while she's praying. She takes entirely too long to get done, so you decide to give her a courtesy fall so she can go away. You've already planned it out—after you fall down and she walks away, you plan to make your way closer to the minister that you want to pray for you. So you won't be so obvious, you pretend to be caught up in deep prayer and worship. Fifteen minutes later, the musicians start to wrap things up and your favorite minister is nowhere to be seen. So, you make your way towards the back of the church, lingering around, hoping that someone will notice you and sense your issue and your desperation. It doesn't happen, so on the ride home, you angrily reason with yourself that you're going to find another church to attend next Sunday because you're tired of going home bound. The pastor has been out of town for the last two Sundays, and you can never seem to get your favorite minister to pray for you. So, you go online and find another church that claims to conduct deliverance. Next Sunday, you find yourself standing at their altar with the pastor himself praying for you. This time, it's got to work! The problem is, his prayer was way too short; this is likely because of the long line of people who are waiting for him to pray for them. You didn't even get a chance to fall before he walked away. And unlike your home church, they don't allow you to linger at the altar. An usher leads you back to your seat, where you sit there disappointed, frustrated, angry and bound! The problem isn't the woman who prayed for you at your home church or the short prayer that the pastor prayed over you at the other church, the problem is, you lack understanding. Consequently, you are placing the burden of your deliverance on other people, rather than accepting that you need to change your ways. Demonic residue is not an invisible substance or scent that follows you around! It is residual thinking! In other words, it's some of those thought-patterns and beliefs that you haven't gotten free from yet. And getting free doesn't mean that you need somebody to lay hands on you; it simply means that you haven't changed your mind in that particular area of your life.

I've come across women who've talked about having been abstinent for five, seven and ten years, only to find themselves falling into sexual immorality with some guy at their local churches. They were hurt and confused as to how this could happen. In many of those cases, the guys had dumped them after one or more sexual encounters with them, and they were angry, humiliated and regretful of the decisions they'd made. They'd had a great testimony; they'd accomplished a marvelous feat by being abstinent for so long, only to give it up to some guy who turned out to be a hypocrite. But what they didn't realize was that they still had demonic residue attached to them from their previous seasons; in other words, they were still in the hallway between two seasons! And the men who approached them saw a familiar pattern. Of all the women at the church, they'd focused on them because there was something about them that made them stand out from the crowd. Not knowing what it was, they pursued and overtook them. Did they see a black cloud of smoke surrounding them? No. Did they smell a spiritual fragrance that caused them to be captivated by the women? No. They saw what they could relate to! Demonic residue manifests itself:

1. In the way that we talk.
2. In the things that we say.
3. In the ways that we walk.
4. Through our mannerisms.
5. In the people who we hang around.
6. In our choices.
7. In the way we respond to conflict.
8. In the way that we dress.
9. In the way that we use our bodies to communicate with people (through eye contact, facial expressions, body language and our movements).
10. Through what we're drawn to or entertained by.

Yes, some guy can pass you in the mall and immediately find himself drawn to you, but it's not an invisible glow or smell that's attracting him. Your demons aren't waving at his demons! No, he's looking at the way you walk or carry yourself. Your eyes tell him what he needs to know about you. Your clothes say a lot! Everything about you communicates, whether you realize this or not! Why do you think a serial killer can walk into a room filled with people and pick out a single woman in that room to attack? Yes, it often is spiritual, but the communication between two unclean spirits isn't always audible! In most cases, it manifests through expressions or behavioral patterns. So, he may find himself watching that woman for more than an hour. Why? Because he's looking at her eyes; he's looking at how she engages people. He's intelligent and he's learned how to spot prey or people who are bound by fear and insecurity. He notices that she avoids eye contact in most cases, and she withdraws herself to a corner quite often. He learns who she has a crush on by tracing her gaze or following her eyes a few times. He realizes that she's insecure and she's clearly all alone at the party, so he sizes her up before finally making his way over to her. His objective is to either gain her trust or find some way to get her intoxicated. Either way, he's picked her out as his next victim, and he's determined not to leave that party until she's in the passenger's seat or the trunk of his car. Again, there is no "aura" surrounding her that attracts him to her; demons look for patterns, movements and behaviors! Can demons communicate through telepathy? Probably! There are situations like the one that happened to my uncle, where he was shot by a cop; his son was shot by his mother's boyfriend, and his son's son died three months after he was born. These are not mere coincidences; Satan can and does use people to carry out his evil agenda, and all too often, he communicates with them through thought-patterns. That cop who stood in front of my uncle likely had a bunch of ungodly thoughts bombarding his mind that day. Maybe, the spirit of fear was harassing him; then again, maybe fear, hatred and anger all came together to create a murderous and tormenting sound that could only be silenced by the sound of gunshots. The cop who killed George Floyd was definitely being used by the enemy! These attacks aren't random! Somebody, somewhere in the bloodline played with witchcraft, not realizing that witchcraft is a demonic contract, and all contracts have small print that most of us don't think to read. When someone is brokenhearted and standing in front of a witch, that person isn't thinking about the repercussions of his or her actions; that person is thinking about relief or revenge! And because many of our ancestors were ignorant regarding the consequences of their actions, they turned to witches and witchcraft for answers! Yes, the enemy is strategic! Yes, you can be on the devil's hit list! Then again, most attacks are random. This is why 1 Peter 5:8 says, "Be sober, be vigilant; because your adversary the devil, as a roaring lion, walketh about, seeking whom he may devour." Satan randomly walks around looking for someone to attack; this tells us that he cannot attack everybody! What is he looking for? Fear. Worry. Doubt. Unforgiveness. Idolatry. Envy. He's looking for what belongs to him, after all, demonic residue is nothing but demon food!

As an entrepreneur who works with ministries, I sometimes speak with believers who still have the residue from their last seasons on them. Most of my clients are good, Godly men and women who are integral, but I do come across people who play mind games in their attempts to get a discount or a freebie. I can almost always tell when I'm dealing with a

224

manipulative client based on the direction that they take and the language that they use. For example, a manipulative person hates protocol; remember, bound people hate boundaries! They also hate systems, order and processes! So, a not-so-integral customer may go to my website and see my company's 800 number on the screen, but decide that he doesn't want to call me. He wants me to call him. He'll then go to the contact page and fill out the form. If I don't call him back, he'll go back to the page and fill out the form again and again. You may ask, "Why is he doing this?" To bring me on his terms; every entrepreneur is either familiar with this tactic or has gone out of business because they haven't familiarized themselves with the tactics of manipulators. When I finally call him back, he'll point out a logo that he wants on my site, but the problem is, he has to pay for it first. Not wanting to pay, he keeps trying to find his way around my system. So, after pointing out the design, he'll start telling me the text that he wants me to put on the design. When this happens, I always interrupt the client and tell him that he has to pay for the design first before we make any modifications to it. In one hundred percent of those cases, the client will respond with, "I know that. I'm just telling you what I want on the design to make sure that you can get it on the design." I then confirm that the text can fit. The client will then talk nonstop, not stopping to let me ask questions or correct something he's said. I then have to barge into the conversation because the client is speaking fast and trying to give himself a discount. He'll be looking at a logo that costs, for example, $179, and he'll say, "So, the logo is $149. Hold on! I'm just writing it down so when I come back to buy it, I'll have the money ready." I have to then talk over him because he's not going to let me speak. "No sir! That's $179, not $149." The client will then say, "Oh, I thought it was $149. I guess I need to put on my glasses. Do you offer any discounts? Do I get two logos for that price?" Believe it or not, this is a conversation that I have quite often! The client is bobbing and weaving his way through the conversation, trying to avoid the truth so he can get a discount. This never happens and I run some of them off because I start dismantling their system while they are talking to me. People like this are damaged or their growth has been stunted in their financial states. I can see it in the way that they talk, the way that they reason and the direction they came in! Bound people always look for windows and cracks to slither through! John 10:1 reads, "Most assuredly, I say to you, he who does not enter the sheepfold by the door, but climbs up some other way, the same is a thief and a robber." Of course, in this scripture, Jesus was dealing with false shepherds, but this scripture, like most of what we read in the Bible, is multidimensional, meaning, it can be applied to many areas of our lives. In other words, people who try to find their way around the doors (legal points of access) are up to no good! Sure, they may be Christians, but the Bible tells us to examine their fruit! And when you find bad fruit in certain states of the human, please know that this doesn't mean that he or she is a bad person. It is a red flag that is designed to warn you about the person's integrity in that particular area. Of course, it can and often does indicate that the individual lacks integrity in other areas because, remember, the enemy will advance from whatever state he's in into other areas of the soul until he's fully bound that individual. But in some cases, it's just demonic residue. This is oftentimes because the person in question is still surrounded by a certain mindset, not just the way that he reasons, but that person hasn't made any new friends. His world is very small, so consequently, he's small-minded. He's manipulative because he's mastered that particular region of thought, and he's been marinating in that world for most, if not all of his life. So, to change his mind, he needs to invest in a lot of books and go outside of the culture and the circles that he's familiar with. This is so that he can become acclimated with another world. Small-minded believers are oftentimes very religious, prideful, rigid and ignorant—and by ignorant, I don't mean stupid. The word "ignorant" comes from the root word "ignore." It means that the truth is available, but they choose to ignore it. This is oftentimes because the truth would destroy what they've built or force them to admit where they're wrong. And because they're prideful, they'd rather stay stuck and broke than to repent and grow! They'd rather remain teachers in one season, rather than become students of another.

Demonic residue is sticky; in other words, it attracts like-minded people, so when you notice that you are surrounded by or still attracting certain types of people, you don't need to track down your favorite minister to ask for prayer. You don't have to give a courtesy fall at your church's altar whenever you don't get the prayer partner that you want. Sure, get prayer because it can and does help! What you have to do is get purged from the old information so that you can make room for new information. In other words, you have to reject a lot of what you've been taught. You do this by investing in and reading books, going to church every Sunday, reading your Bible daily, prayer, going to seminars and conferences and getting yourself a mentor for those areas that you are unlearned in! When you do this, the old mindset will slowly begin to fall away as your new mindset emerges; this will cause the wrong people to evict themselves from your life and the right people to enter your life.

THE POWER OF YES

I wanted to deal with the topic of curses and demonic residue because it is important that you understand these topics when you're setting and enforcing boundaries. If you spiritualize everything, you won't take the necessary steps toward deliverance; instead, you'll become religious and begin to relegate the responsibility of your freedom to others. In other words, you'll stay where you are and use the ministry of deliverance as a toilet and a shower of sorts. Consequently, you'll keep going in circles and cycles until you truly get the wisdom and revelation you need to move forward.

When talking about boundaries, we often talk about the power of the word "no," and of course, this word is a boundary within itself. It reveals the character and the wounds of the people you say it to and it clears the path between two seasons. Most of the people who get in your way are folks you've made agreements with. Most of the issues that block you or get in your way are issues that you haven't drawn or enforced a boundary around; these are issues that you haven't necessarily said "no" to, so the word "no" is definitely one of the most effective weapons in your toolbox (outside of the Word of God). Nevertheless, as powerful as "no" is, the most powerful word you can say (outside of the Word of God) is "yes." Amazingly enough, the word "yes" comes from the Old English word "gise" or "gese" and it means "so be it." In other words, it has the same meaning as the word "amen." So, when you say "yes" to something or someone, you're pretty much saying, "So, be it unto me." I don't think that this is the problem, however. The larger problem lies in the fact that you may not fully understand what you're agreeing to. This makes me think about a dream I had in 2015. In the dream, I was in a large room with a bunch of people, and there was a piano in the room. I don't remember the beginning of the dream, but what I do remember is standing around, talking with the people before everyone went on the run from a very large snake. I was upset at the fact that we were running from it, because I knew that we could all overpower it if we attacked it together. Nevertheless, I ran because everyone else was running. I ended up in an elevator with one or two more people and we pushed the button to go up. Everyone else was somewhere in the building running or hiding from the snake. Some people had gotten onto other elevators; we were all just scattered about the building. Note: it was a corporate space and it was beautiful! Anyhow, while in the elevator, I expressed my concerns to the person or people who were sharing the elevator with me. "Why are we running?" I asked. "If we all come together, we can take the snake!" But I didn't get a response. The door opened and I somehow knew that we were on the top floor of the building. I don't remember too much about that floor, but what I do remember is that we felt uncomfortable in the room we were trying to hide in, so we decided to go to another floor. But as we were coming out of the room and into a hallway, I noticed a door that was slightly ajar. I somehow knew that it was the manager's office and we weren't allowed in that room. The person who was with me decided that he wanted to speak with the manager. I warned him not to go into the room, reminding him that we weren't allowed in that space. He didn't listen. He was upset and he was determined to get the manager involved. I remember watching the door open and I could see an old manager of mine sitting behind a desk. He looked up at the guy who was entering the office before the door closed behind the guy. Almost immediately, the guy came out of the office and I knew that he had been fired, so I left and got on the elevator to go back to the main floor. One by one, I ran into people who'd all run off and we went into the main room where the piano was. That's when I gave my speech. "Why are we running from this thing?! If we stick together, we can kill it!" The people were excited, encouraged and rejuvenated. They seemed to be ready for the fight ahead. That is, until the closet door opened, revealing the snake's head. I don't remember if I'd decapitated him in that moment or if it had been earlier. I think it was earlier. If I remember correctly, the first time the snake had come after us, I'd decapitated it, but I was surprised that the snake hadn't died. It still managed to use fear to scatter the people. Anyhow, when the closet door opened, I saw the snake's head. Immediately, the people froze with fear. That's when the snake began to speak. It told the people, "You know I'm going to catch you! You can't get away from me, so you might as well stop running. If you stop running now, I'll have mercy on you. It then came off the top shelf and rested on the closet's floor, where it opened its mouth and a light came out. One by one, I watched the people walk into the snake's mouth, disappearing into the light. I tried to wake them up; I yelled at them, but they wouldn't listen. Instead, they were terrified of the snake's potential, so they believed him when he said he'd have mercy on them. A few seconds later, it came out of the closet, and that's when I attacked it again. I sat on its head, took a screwdriver and began to gouge out its eyes. The snake kept begging for mercy, but I didn't get up. I kept stabbing away at it.

Was the dream about me? No. Even though I was in the dream, the dream dealt with division. The people of God stood together in good times, but as soon as the enemy came, they scattered. The floors of the building represented rank and responsibility. Again, even though I was in the dream, the dream wasn't necessarily a personal one; it wasn't about my calling or my rank. The top floor represented leadership. To whom much is given, much is required. Me and one or two other people went to the top floor and became uncomfortable because we were safe while everyone else was running around terrified. While me and one of the guys were about to leave the top floor and go back to the main floor, that's when we saw the manager's office; the door was slightly ajar and I could see my former boss in there, but in the dream, he was still my boss. That man represented God and the room He was in represented a legality. The man walking with me decided to go past that door or legality, even though we weren't allowed to go into that space. I tried to warn him, but because he was so frustrated and emotional, he would not listen. He tried to take emotion and logic into a spiritual space. Seconds later, he walked out of the room without a job. In other words, he was stripped of his rank or assignment. I then entered the elevator alone and went back to the main floor. I started meeting back up with the people and we all united in the main room. I started encouraging the people, and they were edified. This represents leadership. It wasn't about me per-se, it was about leaders gathering the sheep together and empowering them. That's when the closet door opened and we saw the snake's head. The closet represents secrets or a hidden place. The snake's head was on a shelf (if I remember correctly). This represents rank. It was in the lowest part of the building (main floor), but on the top shelf. It started lying to the people, and after it was done, it lowered itself to the floor. This represents false humility. The snake opened its mouth, and released a blinding bright light. Of course, we know that this is false light or lies. Behold, Satan does disguise himself as an angel of light! One by one, the people disappeared into the snake's mouth! This is the "yes" they gave him; this represents an agreement! They were devoured by a defeated foe; his head had already been decapitated. He was defeated! But how was he still moving around and talking? That's easy. He drew his power from fear. The people energized a defeated devil. This makes me think of those giant cockroaches that would come into our house at night if we opened the door and didn't close it fast enough. One of my parents would kill the bug, and while its lifeless body was on the floor, they would tell us not to stare at the bug. They said that doing so would make it come alive again. While this wasn't true (it was a superstitious belief), the point they were making was this—what you give your attention to, you empower or give life to.

And finally, I sat on the snake's head. This represents dominion. I brought the enemy under me. Again, I want to reiterate that the dream wasn't casting me as some super-saint that would save the world. No! I represented leadership! Leaders are supposed to gather the flock and deal with the many schisms that separate us! I took dominion over the snake and then began to stab it with a screwdriver. This was an unorthodox weapon. The devil had been defeated, but what I (or leadership) was doing was blinding the snake. This is important because it dealt with clairvoyance or, better yet, false prophecies or false prophets. The snake told the people that it would have mercy on them if they surrendered to it. Obviously, it was lying.

What you say "yes" to is far more powerful than what you say "no" to. Most people who want to learn more about boundary-setting are looking for ways to keep evil people at bay. Some people attempt to use boundaries to tame the folks in their lives, while others use boundaries in an attempt to put people on punishment. Because of this, they almost always end up experiencing high levels of warfare every time they attempt to "train" or "punish" the people in their lives. This is because Satan cannot be domesticated. Boundaries are invisible lines that the enemy can clearly see! And when he sees them in a place where he has some measure of rule or dominion, he typically responds violently! Boundaries have to be solid; they cannot be fluid, nor can they be erasable or optional. They have to be set in stone, meaning, they can't have any give to them! A good example to consider is this—a woman puts her abusive boyfriend out of her house. She even has him arrested. Nevertheless, three days later, she goes down to the jailhouse and bails him out. He returns to the house and brings all of his belongings back with him. The two have clearly reconciled; that is, until the next fight. The woman calls the cops again after her boyfriend blacks her eye. The cops arrest him, and a few days later, she shows back up at the jail with her cashed paycheck in her hands. She has him arrested again and again, and she bails him out again and again. All the same, every time they go to court, she lies so that the charges against her boyfriend can be dropped. Because of this, the police stop taking her calls seriously. One day, she calls the cops and asks for an officer to be dispatched to her home once again. Nevertheless, she's made an enemy out of the entire police force. They have to do their jobs and go out to her residence, but because of her pattern of behavior, they don't take the call too seriously, after all, it's clear to them that she's using the system in an attempt to punish or train her boyfriend. Two officers arrive at her apartment and knock on the door thirty minutes after the call came in, but she doesn't answer the door. They knock a few more times, but still, no answer. They reason within themselves that she's clearly made up with her boyfriend and no longer need their assistance, after all, she has done this before. What they don't realize is that she's inside the apartment with a single gunshot wound to her head, bleeding to death. Two hours later, she gives up the ghost, and her body isn't discovered until two weeks later after her neighbors complain about a foul odor coming from her apartment. What happened here? Her boundaries were false. They were mirages; they had been designed to give off the illusion that she wouldn't keep tolerating the boyfriend's ways, but they really didn't exist. They only served to provoke him all the more, so he took her life. Honestly, this is a story that's more common than we want to admit. What she'd said "yes" to (the relationship) was far more powerful than what she'd said "no" to (abuse, cheating, etc.) Her "yes" represented the legality; it was what the enemy needed to steal her life. Think about it this way. Most of us have a relative or two who is a thief. He'd steal anything that isn't bolted down if he could. Because he has "sticky fingers," we don't invite him into our personal space (homes). This is because inviting him in means that we have to monitor his movements closely. However, because he doesn't have any physical access to us, he cannot and does not steal from us. Do you see where this is going? Satan can only steal what he has access to. Again, oftentimes people say "yes" to relationships, partnerships and the like, not realizing fully what they are agreeing to! Amos 3:3 reads, "Can two walk together, except they be agreed?" The phrase "walk together" deals with agreement, but it also deals with direction. Who you agree with or walk with determines or is determined by the direction you're heading in. If I partner up (through marriage) with an unsaved man, first off, it would be clear that we're standing on the wrong foundation, even though I'm a believer. We wouldn't be standing on the Word since the Word told me to not unequally yoke myself with an unbeliever. So, the foundation would likely be immaturity, lust, trauma, rebellion or impatience. These are all faulty foundations that cannot and will not stand the tests of time. When a house has foundational issues, the walls begin to crack in some places, the doors begin to stick and the house becomes unstable. Additionally, a bad foundation can cause:

1. Additional damage to the house's structure
2. Plumbing issues
3. Water damage
4. Mold and mildew
5. Insect infestations
6. Increase in utility bills

As it is in the natural, so it is in the spirit! Foundations tend to get damaged when the ground underneath them shifts! The word "ground" here means legal footing. Ephesians 4:27 reads, "Neither give place to the devil." The word "place" in this text means "grounds" or "opportunity." What causes the ground underneath a physical structure to shift is normally when the soil becomes unstable. This is oftentimes the result of bedrock erosion, the faulting of bedrocks, earthquakes, the formation of sinkholes, soil compaction or loess deposits.

The following was taken from Encyclopedia Britannica. "Loess, an unstratified, geologically recent deposit of silty or loamy material that is usually buff or yellowish brown in color and is chiefly deposited by the wind. Loess is a sedimentary deposit composed largely of silt-size grains that are loosely cemented by calcium carbonate. It is usually homogeneous and highly porous and is traversed by vertical capillaries that permit the sediment to fracture and form vertical bluffs. The word loess, with connotations of origin by wind-deposited accumulation, is of German origin and means 'loose.'" So, if I married an unsaved man, we'd start building on an unstable foundation; that foundation would be resting on unstable grounds. These are the same grounds I'd use to file for divorce! My "yes" to the man would eventually give up its ghost, and before long, I'd find myself agreeing with God; before long, I'd find myself saying "no" to that relationship because it was unequally yoked.

I've counseled a LOT of broken people. They were heartbroken, not realizing that their hearts weren't the first things to break. The foundations that they stood on with the folks who broke their hearts had cracked because those foundations were unstable. Eventually, the house that had been divided did not and could no longer stand, and they were heartbroken as a result of this. Most of these beautiful, but broken souls talked about the many storms, betrayals, rejections and traumas they'd experienced, mostly starting at home with their parents, and then bleeding over into other areas of their lives relationally. Unbeknownst to them, they were doing the spiritual equivalent of cutting themselves. They did this by:

1. Not taking accountability for what happened to the adult-sized version of themselves.
2. Refusing to forgive the people who hurt them.
3. Refusing to let go of the fantasies they have regarding the people who hurt them, including their parents, lovers and former lovers.
4. Refusing to close the doors between themselves and toxic people or, at minimum, repositioning those people in their lives.
5. Refusing to establish and enforce boundaries in their lives.

This is spiritual cutting because what they were doing was holding onto broken people and constantly getting cut in the process. There's an adage or concept around that's been circulating for years (I don't remember the actual words), but the gist of it is this—toxic people are like broken glass. If you touch them, you will get cut. The short of it is, you can hurt yourself trying to help some people. Of course, I'm not telling you to avoid broken people. I am, however, suggesting that you help those who want to be helped, but don't hurt yourself trying to help people who like being the way that they are! If they've said "yes" to a mentality or reality that's toxic to your existence, you have to place a "no" or a boundary between you and those people. It is possible that you may never have parents who you can brag about, it is possible that you may never have a close relationship with your family, and it is possible that you may never have an amicable relationship with the father or mother of your children. This is because these people have the ability to make choices, and God does not infringe upon that ability. Nevertheless, you can avoid having a toxic relationship with them by setting and establishing boundaries and making it a point to not engage in any toxic conversations that they try to initiate or instigate. The hard truth is, some people are way too toxic for you to be personally affiliated with. It is always a good practice to examine the toxicity level of a person to determine how much (if any) access that person can have to you. All the same, it is unwise to allow yourself to become angry or to internalize the fact that someone you know and love is unapologetically toxic. Getting upset with a toxic person for being manipulative and narcissistic is no better than getting upset with a person for being schizophrenic. People become what they've been exposed to and they become what they've made peace with. Now, it's your turn. Make peace with the fact that you may have to love some people from a distance.

And then, of course, there's the other side of "yes." This is where we agree to do something that is beneficial to our spiritual and mental health. For example, when I gave my life to the Lord at the age of 21, I entered into an agreement (covenant) with Him. Nevertheless, I was a babe in Christ and all I knew was sin. I'd spent the entirety of my young life surrounded and influenced by toxic people, with a few normal folks sprinkled in here and there. So, my "yes" to God was just as unstable as I was, but thankfully, God had already created a grace account for me—one that I could never overdraft. It took me several years of falling and failing to get to where I am now. I learned that God didn't mind the slip-ups because He knew that I wasn't going to get it right overnight. The more I said "yes" to Him, the more I said "no" to who I used to be and how I used to be. Slowly, but surely, the people who were in my life began to fall away. Eventually, I stopped trying to fix or mend those relationships. I simply stood on the sidelines and watched them slip away. I'd said "yes" to God and I wasn't about to retract it!

Every time you say "yes" to the Lord, He will give you a tour of His heart; He'll show you a side of Himself that you've never seen. The more you agree with Him, the more He'll reveal to you. He's always excited to show Himself off because He knows that He's good and He knows that everything you've been looking for is in Him! Think about how the father of the prodigal son felt when his son returned home. Jesus told the story in Luke 15:11-32, and it reads, "There was a man who had two sons. And the younger of them said to his father, 'Father, give me the share of property that is coming to me.' And he divided his property between them. Not many days later, the younger son gathered all he had and took a journey into a far country, and there he squandered his property in reckless living. And when he had spent everything, a severe famine arose in that country, and he began to be in need. So he went and hired himself out to one of the citizens of that country, who sent him into his fields to feed pigs. And he was longing to be fed with the pods that the pigs ate, and no one gave him anything. But when he came to himself, he said, 'How many of my father's hired servants have more than enough bread, but I perish here with hunger! I will arise and go to my father, and I will say to him, 'Father, I have sinned against heaven and before you. I am no longer worthy to be called your son. Treat me as one of your hired servants." And he arose and came to his father. But while he was still a long way off, his father saw him and felt compassion, and ran and embraced him and kissed him. And the son said to him, Father, I have sinned against heaven and before you. I am no longer worthy to be called your son. But the father said to his servants, 'Bring quickly the best robe, and put it on him, and put a ring on his hand, and shoes on his feet. And bring the fattened calf and kill it, and let us eat and celebrate. For this my son was dead, and is alive again; he was lost, and is found.' And they began to celebrate. Now his older son was in the field, and as he came and drew near to the house, he heard music and dancing. And he called one of the servants and asked what these things meant. And he said to him, 'Your brother has come, and your father has killed the fattened calf, because he has received him back safe and sound.' But he was angry and refused to go in. His father came out and entreated him, but he answered his father, 'Look, these many years I have served you, and I never disobeyed your command, yet you never gave me a young goat, that I might celebrate with my friends. But when this son of yours came, who has devoured your property with prostitutes, you killed the fattened calf for him!' And he said to him, 'Son, you are always with me, and all that is mine is yours. It was fitting to celebrate and be glad, for this your brother was dead, and is alive; he was lost, and is found.'"

This is a picture of how God feels about you! When you knock on His heart, He answers with excitement! When you open your ears to Him, He talks nonstop because of how happy He is to hear from you! When you call on His name, He's more than happy to answer! Your "yes" provokes Heaven to open its windows; your "yes" causes the season you're in to spit you out! This is what Jonah's "yes" did for him! His "yes" caused what was the equivalent of a demonic agent (the great fish) to spit him out. To spit out, spirituality speaking, means to renounce. It means that the great fish no longer had the legal grounds to hold him.

You'd be amazed at how drastically one "yes" could change your life; that is, for the better or the worse. One "yes":

1. Caused Adam and Eve to sin against the Most High God, thus, condemning them and all of mankind.
2. Caused the people of the Earth to turn against God; consequently, suffering the fate of the Great Flood that destroyed every living creature except Noah, his family and the animals that were aboard the ark with them.
3. Caused Abram to sleep with his wife's handmaid, Hagar, and produce Ishmael.
4. Caused Sodom and Gomorrah to be utterly

destroyed.

5. Caused Esau to sell his birthright for a bowl of soup.
6. Caused Joseph's brothers to plot and ultimately sell him into slavery.
7. Caused many of the Israelites to fall in the wilderness before they could reach the promised land.
8. Caused Orpah (Ruth's daughter-in-law) to return to the vomit (system) she'd been delivered from.
9. Caused Samson to lose his eyes and his strength, and ultimately die by suicide.
10. Caused David to sleep with another man's wife, have that man killed, and then, proceed to marry his wife.

On the other side of the spectrum, one "yes":

1. Caused Noah to build an ark to save his family.
2. Caused Abraham to become the father of all nations.
3. Caused Job to defeat the enemy and recover all that the enemy had stolen from him.
4. Led Jacob on a mission where he'd go and grow from being Jacob to Israel.
5. Got Joseph into the castle, where he served as Pharaoh's right-hand man.
6. Caused Moses to take up the charge of leading God's people out of Egypt.
7. Caused Ruth to be named in the Bible. Jesus is a part of her lineage!
8. Caused David to stay the course, and eventually become a man after God's own heart.
9. Caused 12 men to follow Jesus, even when it wasn't

popular to do so.
10. Saved us from eternal damnation!

Your "yes" to one world is your "no" to another. Your "yes" to one system is your departure from another. We talked about the hallway between two seasons; this is the wilderness, grace or space that God gives you to walk off the residue of your last season. He also allows you to preview/sample your next season. One of the most common mistakes people tend to make while in this space is they keep trying to marry or blend their old season with their next season. If each season had handlebars, you'd see them standing between the two, using all of their emotional and physical strength to pull those seasons together. Of course, they'd fail and you'd see them throwing a bunch of religious temper tantrums. The issue is, you cannot mix seasons! The Israelites could not drag Egypt into their promised land, and God wouldn't let them enter the promised land with an Egyptian mindset. They had to leave one place to enter the other; they had to renounce one mindset to embrace another. To break a generational curse, you have to say "no" to Satan's will and "yes" to the will of God. To get all of the demonic residue out of you, you have to repeatedly say "yes" to God and "no" to the enemy. Because God gave you a gift called "will" and He gave you the freedom to exercise that will, He allows you to make the choices you want to make, but you can't choose the consequences. Every choice you make is part of a system and a sequence. The word "sequence" means a connected order of events, a succession or a domino effect.

I'll go as far to say that every choice you make is part of a domino effect, stemming from other choices you've made or choices your parents, grandparents, ancestors or someone who's had any measure of influence in your life has made. And every sequence is followed by a consequence; that is, an action that takes place in direct response to your choice; this is called a reaction. This is why the most important boundaries you'll ever have to set are around yourself; that is, exercising your will to do what's right, even when you're tempted to do otherwise!

Challenge yourself this way—write down your greatest dreams or desires. I'm not talking about what life has taught you to settle for. I'm talking about the life you'd establish for yourself if you could have it. While doing this, be cognizant of what you're writing. Ask yourself, "Am I settling? Am I just writing this down because I feel that it's within reach or seems doable?" The reason this is important is because the average person's dreams are nothing but a group of settlements they've reached and subconsciously agreed to because they don't have enough faith to believe God for bigger. If it's something you're settling for, scratch it off the list and write down what you'd love to have. Once you're done, take that list and rip it up into tiny pieces. Why are you doing this? It's simple. Even your grandest plans don't match God's plans for you! All the same, you have to give up your plans to access God's plans. Next, write down five new boundaries that you're going to set around yourself in every area of your life. Don't forget to enforce these boundaries.

Additionally, every boundary has to have a consequence or penalty attached to it. For example, if you set boundaries around yourself, you have to penalize yourself should you go outside these boundaries. A great penalty is donating money to a good cause! And you can't donate a small amount; it needs to be substantial enough to impact you! So you could say, for example, that if you go on your ex's social media pages, you will give one hundred dollars to St. Jude's Hospital. Be sure that you're accountable with this and be sure to follow through! If you keep doing this, slowly but surely, you'll become more disciplined, a whole lot bolder and best of all, wiser!

Say "yes" to God; in other words, submit to His will for you. Say "no" to Satan; in other words, don't do what you're tempted to do. Instead, do what you're designed to do! All of Heaven is rooting for you! All God needs is your "yes" and the rest will someday be history! Let's grow forward!

A NOTE TO THE EMPATH AND THE PROPHETIC INDIVIDUAL

Look at the spectrum below.

Victim	Survivor	Overcomer	More than a Conqueror

In this model, you see the four temperatures of faith as it relates to someone who's been hurt, traumatized, rejected or abandoned. I created this model to identify and measure the growth of the people I've counseled, coached or mentored. This spectrum allows me to give the individual the tools he or she needs to move to the next level. Let's look at the four levels or mentalities.

Victim

This is the individual who has been hurt and is still feeling or living through the effects of that pain. I spoke to a logo client of mine some years ago, and even though the woman had called to share with me what she wanted on her logo, somehow, the conversation had taken another turn. She started telling me about her ex-husband. He'd left and divorced her for someone else, leaving her to raise their child alone. She was hurt and angry, and I was SURE that she was nursing a fresh wound, meaning, I was confident that the wound was no more than a year old. I was going through a divorce, so I understood her pain and her frustration, nevertheless, I did not understand her anger. This is because I'd made a CONSCIOUS choice to forgive my ex. I just had to get the Holy Spirit involved to aid me in this process. Howbeit, as I spoke with this woman, I realized that she needed to not only forgive her ex, but she needed to get some therapy behind the event. I listened intently for more than an hour as she detailed how she'd been financially crippled by her ex's decision to walk away from their family. She then began to speak evil over him, saying that his marriage was going to end, and everything he put his hands to was going to fail. I tried to encourage her, and at the same time, I began to cancel her words under my breath. I made a mental note to pray for her ex-husband because it was clear to me that she had spent a great deal of time speaking curses over him. She claimed that God had told her that the man's marriage would fail and that he would suffer because of what he'd done to her. After encouraging her and praying with her, I got off the line. The next day, she called again so that we could discuss her logo order, and once again, she started talking about her ex. God then laid it on my heart to ask her how long it had been since he'd walked away from their family. Imagine my surprise when she said ten years ago. TEN YEARS AGO?! I was SURE that her wound was fresh because of the anger, the bitterness and the rawness that she spoke with. There I was going through a divorce, and I was the one doing the counseling! And if that wasn't shocking enough, what really caught me off guard was when she told me that the woman he was married to was not the same woman he'd divorced her to be with. His former relationship had failed; he'd moved on and married someone else. Nevertheless, she was still so angry with him that she didn't want to see him prosper in anything! She even blamed him for the fact that she was struggling financially. This is what we call the victim. I shared that story so that you can understand that there is no timeline on any of these categories. You have to grow out of them by intentionally doing the hard work needed to forgive the person or the people who've hurt you. This has to be a decision that you make even while in the midst of your pain!

The victim mentality is a calling card for narcissists! For example, if your mother was narcissistic, controlling and manipulative, chances are, you'll find yourself attracted to a partner who's also narcissistic, controlling and manipulative. What would attract you to this person would be the fact that he or she knows how to stand up to your mother. In other words, your dependency on the narcissist is what will keep attracting that spirit to you; that is, until you finally divorce that devil by divorcing that mindset.

Victims have a lot of sad or sob stories; they focus on two dynamics:
1. What they did right.
2. What others did wrong.

This means that they are limited in their perceptions. If you fit under this category, please note that there is another perspective that you have yet to embrace, and that is God's perspective. I want you to imagine a small lizard. To an ant, that lizard is a BIG problem! But to a cat, that lizard is a toy. It's all a matter of perspective! The reason you're still a victim is because you've shrunk yourself, all the while, magnifying both the person who hurt you and the event itself. To overcome this mentality, you have to forgive the person or people who mishandled you and change your perspective of yourself. God called you more than a conqueror in Christ Jesus, but you have to learn to see yourself this way. In other words, you first have to STOP surrounding yourself with predatory people, being overly giving to those people, and then playing the victim every time they prove themselves to be predatory. There's something they have that you want, which makes them just as much a victim of yours as you are a victim of theirs. It's all about codependency! You have to see both sides of the spectrum, otherwise, you'll keep seeing yourself as a victim, and consequently, you'll evoke one of the laws of nature. We call this the "food chain." Google defines the term "food chain" this way: "a hierarchical series of organisms each dependent on the next as a source of food." On this spectrum, the victim is on the lowest end; in other words, the victim is what's on the menu! This means that you'll keep attracting predatory people to you until you stop thinking, reasoning and seeing yourself as a victim.

Note: whenever we've been hurt, we immediately become victims, and this is okay, but you shouldn't stay there. I used to bring victims close to me until I noticed a pattern. I realized that while they had many stories of constantly being mishandled, misused and misguided, most of them who'd mastered those regions of thoughts (seasons) had little to no intention of coming out of them. They just wanted someone to talk to about the events that were taking place or had taken place in their lives, but they didn't necessarily want to heal or break free from their oppressors. I came to realize that I was just another character that they'd added to their stories, and I also saw another pattern. Many victims are just as (if not more) manipulative than the narcissists who control and manipulate them. Many people stuck in this region of thought would tell their counselors or coaches about what their villains had done to them on any given day. They'd relieve themselves by talking nonstop about all they'd done for their villains, how they'd stuck by them when everyone told them to leave and they'd update their coaches or counselors on the villain/narcissist's latest antics. After that, they'd listen as the coach/counselor advised them, but in truth, they really didn't want this advice. Listening to twenty and thirty minutes of advice was just the price they had to pay for having human toilets. (Of course, this is not all victims, but this is for the ones who are professional victims.) They'd repeatedly interrupt the folks who were giving them advice just to share another tidbit, and if as a coach/counselor, you said something that they felt they could use in their next argument with the narcissist, they'd highlight, write down and memorize that specific phrase. After that, they'd start another fight with their villains and say, for example, "My counselor told me that people like you love to control and manipulate folks, and that I should have disassociated from you a long time ago! But no! I decided to stick around and try to give you another chance!" In other words, the coach, counselor or advisor becomes another tool in their own personal bags of tricks. This means that they too are becoming relatively narcissistic. I've discovered that the goal of the narcissist isn't just to control, manipulate and dominate people, but to reproduce that spirit in others. Empaths eventually become narcissists or they become some degree of narcissistic if and when they don't get the help they need to overcome, not the person of the narcissist, but the spirit behind narcissism (Jezebel). To overcome Jezebel, the have to overcome the fruit of narcissism, which is idolatry and witchcraft.

The Survivor

Imagine that a woman was in a boat on a river. All of a sudden, the boat flipped over and she found herself being pulled by the river's current. "I can't swim!" she shouts as the current pulls her towards utter destruction. And just as she feels herself losing consciousness, she suddenly feels a man wrapping his arms around her and pulling her to safety. While she's in the river, she's a victim. The minute she is pulled out of that river, she becomes a survivor. When the paramedics come, she will share her story with them. When the news anchors show up, she will share her story with them. She will do all of this while wrapped up in a blanket and trembling. In that moment and in that hour, she is a survivor, and as such, she will be afraid to get back in a boat. Howbeit, she won't be afraid to share her story.

Survivors are professional victims who've learned to see life from a shoreline experience. They can still see the rivers that tried to drown them, but they are no longer in those rivers. They still tremble around water because, to them, the experience is relatively fresh enough for them to recall, but distant enough for them to only remember some of the details surrounding it. The survivor is what the media popularizes today; they can give a Ted Talk about their experiences and what they've learned from those experiences, but they still haven't learned how to swim. In other words, they are out of the rivers, but they haven't defeated them. They can simply articulate what they've gone through in a way that helps others to relate to their plights. The victim won't return to the river, but the survivor will. Nevertheless, the survivor will only get on a boat if a camera is pointed at them, and even then, the survivor will tremble and insist on getting off the boat before it inches into the water. This is because he or she has not overcome the experience; the individual has simply survived it. A woman who's survived a bad relationship, for example, still speaks reproachfully about her ex. Like most victims, she cannot and will not take responsibility for her role in her own hurt. This is because she can only see cause and effect; she remembers her intentions and her efforts, and she remembers how those intentions and efforts were repaid. What she refuses to see, however, is the fact that the relationship should have never taken place. Accountability will make you trace an issue all the way down to its roots, but blame deals with the surface of the issue. I like to describe it this way. If there are weeds growing in my yard, I could hire my lawn guy to come out and cut the grass. From there, my lawn would look amazing, and most folks won't notice the weeds because what I've done is dealt with the aesthetic side of the issue. Nevertheless, if I want my lawn to be free of weeds, I have to deal with the root of the issue. I need to use some weed killer, instead of just dressing up the problem. I say that to say this—survivors focus on the fact that they had weeds (tares) growing in their lives, but they don't focus on the fact that they invited them there. This is why victims and survivors find themselves in a perpetual cycle of defeat; they are always having to overcome something or someone! Nevertheless, many survivors never overcome the issues that plague them; instead, they become professional survivors or professional victims, always sharing yet another story of hurt, rejection and frustration for the world to hear. Survivors like to take pictures of themselves in their shoreline experiences, for example, they'll take a snapshot of themselves lying in hospital beds. One of the problems with the survivor is that they can and sometimes do become addicted to the attention they get every time they survive another river experience. Consequently, the more broken ones will toss themselves into rivers just so they can have something else to share via social media or on their jobs. This, of course, is a form of narcissism, and it is relatively common today.

There is a temptation to settle down in this region of thought, but if you truly want to embrace a whole new reality, you have to embrace a new perspective; that is, you have to embrace a whole new way of thinking.

The Overcomer

This is a great place to be, but it's not the peak of the mountain! What's amazing about the overcomer is that the overcomer didn't just survive the river experience, but the overcomer also overcame the temptation to remain a victim or to operate as a survivor! This is especially true if the overcomer has wrestled with the spirit of rejection. This particular spirit often romanticizes the idea of remaining a victim, and those fantasies have to be wrestled down and decapitated. The overcomer survived the river experience and has left the shorelines behind. In other words, he or she is no longer there! They've moved on! The overcomer has forgiven the person or people who've hurt him or her, and the overcomer has tossed away every opportunity to get vengeance that has ever presented itself to him or her! You see, when Satan decides to ensnare you with unforgiveness, all he has to do is get you to focus on your intentions and your efforts, and then have you contrast that with how the other party responded. But when you ask God to help you forgive the person or the people who've hurt you, He doesn't give you a different feeling towards those people. He gives you a different perspective of those individuals, meaning, He'll give you a bird's eye view of their lives, including their pasts and their present, but Satan will go out of his way to have you to focus on the event itself. Satan creates highlight reels in your imagination to get you to constantly relive conversations and experiences that were hurtful or traumatic. But when he fails at this, and you ask God to help you forgive your enemies, Satan then responds by giving you an opportunity to get vengeance. I call this stage "D-day" or, better yet, Decision Day. This is the moment when you suddenly realize something that the person said or did, or you realize something you can say or do to completely shatter your enemy's reality. This is high-level temptation; it is the moment when you are on the threshold of your deliverance, but the enemy decides to extend to you what I call "the settlement offer."

When you're winning in court or if the defendant decides that you will likely win, chances are, the defendant will offer you a settlement. This settlement is way less than what you stand to win, but it relieves you of having to go through the stress and the strain of testifying and having to show up at court everyday. Satan employs this very tactic. If he sees that you're too zealous or too determined to stay stuck, he'll offer you a settlement. He'll offer you the opportunity to "get even" with the person or the people who, in all truth, were nothing but decoys that he used to break and pervert you. And this settlement often looks really nice, especially if you are afraid of your next season! For example, I was living in Florida in an apartment, and I'd decided to clean the extra bedroom in that apartment. I was halfway through a divorce, I'd forgiven my ex and God was about to show me why He'd pressured me to forgive the guy when He did. Satan sensed that God was about to do something, so while cleaning the room, I found something that my ex had left behind. I picked the item up, and in that moment, I found myself holding his future in my hands. Out of respect for him, I won't say what I found (note: it wasn't anything perverted, illegal or even bad; it was just something that could have potentially cost him his career). Honestly, he hadn't committed a crime; he'd just violated a policy. Right there, my thoughts were interrupted by the voice of the enemy. I suddenly thought about all I'd done for him, and what he'd done to me. I suddenly thought about how he valued his career, and how I could send a powerful message to him by simply making a phone call. That thought process lasted a few seconds before I overrode it with another thought. "I forgive him," I said in my heart. So, I called him and told him what I was holding in my hands. "Come get it," I said to him. "This could get you in a lot of trouble." At first, I could tell that he was relatively suspicious of my intentions, after all, we were going through a divorce and things had initially started off as contentious. He tried to assure me that it wasn't a big deal, but I knew it was. He agreed to come and pick the item up that following day, because he had to come to my apartment anyhow to drop off a package. While in my apartment, he was surprised to see that not only had I forgiven him, I was making a lot of efforts to ensure that I didn't hurt him in any way. I handed him a piece of paper with all of the logins and passwords of his that I had, and told him to change his passwords. I handed him the item that I'd found, and I told him to make sure he followed protocol so that he wouldn't get in any trouble. That day, my ex got saved while sitting on the couch in my living room BECAUSE I was exemplifying the heart and the nature of Christ. In other words, I was an overcomer! "And they overcame him by the blood of the Lamb, and by the word of their testimony; and they loved not their lives unto the death" (Revelation 12:11).

An overcomer can go back to the river, rent another boat and get back on the water. An overcomer is no longer moved by the hurt or the memories of an event, but instead, only shares the details to help others to overcome. This is because they've taken full responsibility for everything that has happened to the adult-sized version of themselves. All the same, they've forgiven the folks who hurt them when they were kids because again, God has given them a different perspective of the event. An overcomer has an eagle's view of the event that he or she survived. Along with survivors, these are the people we celebrate the most at church. They will happily testify about what God has brought them through, and they will also help others to overcome those same rivers (issues). Everything about them radiates with authority; they can tell you about the narcissist (Jezebel spirit) and their experiences with the narcissist, but they will also tell you how they finally stood up for themselves and took back their God-given authority, their identities and their peace. They will also tell you what this decision cost them. And as expensive as it is to finally establish and enforce boundaries, one thing you'll hear (or sense) with an overcomer is that he or she would be willing to pay that price ten thousand times over if he or she had to do it again.

More Than a Conqueror

Romans 8:37: Nay, in all these things we are more than conquerors through him that loved us.

A conqueror fights a war, but someone who is more than a conqueror sits on the sidelines and receives the benefits (and loot) of war without ever having to lift a finger. In other words, this is someone who trusts in and benefits from the finished work of Jesus Christ.

I have a huge burn mark on my left arm that extends from the top of my upper arm almost to my wrist. Thankfully, it isn't bumpy, nor is it raised. It's as smooth as the rest of my skin; it's just darker and it's on the underparts of my arm. This scar was the result of me pulling a pot of boiling sugar-covered peaches on myself when I was two-years old. My mother was making peach cobbler, and she'd pulled the peaches off the stove and sat the pot on the table (for whatever reason). She said she'd turned her back for a few seconds, and when she turned around, she saw me pulling on the pot. She tried to rush over and stop me, but it was too late. I pulled the peaches down and burned my arm and the left side of my torso. I was rushed to the hospital and spent a few days there, and to date, I can still see the dark coloration on my skin, but amazingly enough, they aren't scars, instead, my skin is just darker than the rest in those areas. In other words, my body absorbed the scarred tissue. What's better is that I don't remember the event, so I'm in no way traumatized by it (even though I don't like peach cobbler, not because of the event, but because I've never been a fan of how it tastes). This makes me more than a conqueror. Please understand that being more than a conqueror doesn't mean that you didn't suffer through the traumatic event. It simply means that the event has not scarred you. Someone who is more than a conqueror (in Christ) has survived the event, overcome the trauma and the temptations and have come out on the other side of the event. This person is no longer sitting on the shorelines of the event, and this person is no longer just renting a boat to confront the waters that once tried to claim his or her life. Someone who is more than a conqueror will buy the boat and frequent the river, looking for other folks to pull out of it. This person has learned to swim in what once tried to overwhelm him or her; this person has learned to dominate the currents! This person not only has slain Goliath, but he or she has cut off the head (authority) of Goliath, and is now holding it up for the world to see! This person has stolen Goliath's sword and is now using it to give God the glory!

Which one are you? What is your temperature right now? Being able to locate where you are will help you to move from one region of thought to another. Yes, you may have been raped, abused, neglected, rejected, abandoned and traumatized to no ends, but this does NOT mean that you have to remain there! I often tell people this—vengeance belongs to God, but healing belongs to you! All the same, the best revenge that you can ever get isn't against the people who hurt you, but against the devil in the people who hurt you. You do this by taking the trauma, the fear and all of those raw emotions, and handing them over to God. He then allows you to extract the wisdom and the revelation from each event, and then, He gives you His perspective of the events. This means that you'll become stronger, wiser and more aware of who you are! You have to overcome the desire to win in front of your enemies! Instead, you are to embrace the desire to win on behalf of your enemies! And like me, some of the people who hurt you will get saved just because you chose to forgive them and move beyond what they put you through! This is when you get to take the spoils of war back from the real enemy, Satan!

And to anyone who is trying to help an empath, please note the following:
You can:
- Counsel a victim.
- Coach a survivor.
- Mentor an overcomer.
- Disciple a conqueror.

Counseling is all about giving the person the information and the tools he or she needs to heal, and then, monitoring what that person does with those tools. Not every victim wants to be made whole. In truth, some people love the attention they get from being victims. Coaching, on the other hand, deals with targeting a specific area of a person's life that needs to be developed outside of their emotional health. Coaching is more about growth and development, whereas, counseling is more about healing. Mentorship is centered around leadership; the goal behind mentorship is to help a person master a certain area of his or her life, especially in ministry, business and so on. All of these have to do with levels of intimacy. For example, you can't bring a victim close to you because it's only a matter of time before the victim accuses you of being his or her villain. This is especially true if the victim doesn't have an active villain in his or her life or if the victim suddenly starts embracing someone who doesn't necessarily like you. This isn't to say that all victims are intentionally malicious, but it is to say that victimhood is a state of mind; it is a perspective or a neighborhood of thinking that limits how a person sees the world. It's okay to be a victim immediately after an incident, but if you remain there, the issue goes from being an event to being a stronghold. Lastly, you disciple a conqueror or someone who's more than a conqueror. Discipleship is all about the leader duplicating himself or herself, and also pulling out the raw potential of the person he or she is leading. This means to bring that person close; this way, you can inspect him or her and help to develop that person into the gift he or she was created by God to be!

Note Center

Great day to you and thank you for reading the fifth and final installation of the Book of Boundaries. I pray that the information in this book not only opened your eyes, but that it also gave you the motivation, the insight and the tools you need to set and secure boundaries in your life. And since this is the final book in the series, I decided to create this section to give you more space to document your progress as you navigate through each book and as you navigate through life in general. Use the space provided below to detail some of the lessons you've learned, how you plan to apply them and to journal about your success and failures. Happy boundary-building!

Your Name	
Today's Date	
City, State	

Who are your boundaries designed to protect?
- Name:
- Name:
- Name:
- Name:
- Name:
- Name:
- Name:
- Name:

Use this section to write a letter to the future you. Come back and read this letter anytime you need encouragement or to be reminded why you decided to set and enforce boundaries in your life.

Journal

CCLXXXV

Printed in Great Britain
by Amazon

86629546R00169